Memories that Won't Go Away

A Tribute to the Children of the Kindertransport

Michele M. Gold

Artwork by Gabriella Y. Karin

KIP – Kotarim International Publishing, Ltd.

Edited by: Marian Lebor
Layout, Typesetting and Cover Design by: S. Kim Glassman
Publisher: Moshe Alon
Cover photographs used with permission
Special thanks to the United States Holocaust Memorial Museum
ISBN: 978-965-7589-10-6
Printed in Israel 2014

For the children who had to leave,

for the parents who had the courage to let them go

and for the families and organizations that provided a safe haven.

CONTENTS

PREFACE

The Courageous Anguish of Parents and Their Children

By Michael Berenbaum

*Director of Sigi Ziering Institute and Professor of Jewish Studies
at the American Jewish University, Los Angeles, California*

I can't remember exactly when I first learned the word Kindertransport, but I do clearly remember when I first learned that there had been a concerted effort to save Jewish children from Germany, Austria, Czechoslovakia and Poland and ship them to freedom in England before the war. Charles Feld was a businessman and volunteer cantor, who was active on the board of Camp Ramah, which I attended each summer. He spoke with a peculiar accent: part English, part German and part American. I once asked him about his accent and he told me that he had left his parents and Germany and was sent with his sister to England before the war and raised there. No larger story was told but I remembered, in part because camp represented the voluntary separation from one's parents. We left *for* camp joyfully and would return *from* camp sadly, happy to see our parents but so sad to leave our friends and the camp community behind. Like all children, I could not imagine my parents not being there, not welcoming me. I could not fathom a 'final separation'. Little was said but much was remembered.

Still later, but while still a teenager, I read Arthur Morse's *While Six Million Died*, a damning portrait of American inaction and American-Jewish inaction during the Holocaust, and learned that the Wagner-Rogers Bill to bring 20,000 Jewish children from the countries ruled and occupied by Germany in pre-war 1939 had failed to get out of Committee. It died even before reaching the House and Senate floors, much as many of these children were later to die before reaching freedom. I was ashamed of America, ashamed of the Jewish people in America.

Still later, while a young man, I met Norbert Wolheim, a survivor of Auschwitz, who had helped organize the Kindertransport and was on the last of those transports that reached England just as World War II began. He could have stayed with these children, a free man in a free land, but he chose to return since his wife and his child remained behind in Germany, and he could not contemplate his life without them, his freedom without them. Courage took many forms during those dark years, and Norbert's courage to return demonstrated his love and his integrity. A simple act – it may have also been heroic – but he could not have done otherwise. It was, as my children might say, 'a no-brainer'.

Finally, I had heard the name 'Kindertransport'.

Years later, I encountered the experience of these children directly and profoundly. Deborah Oppenheimer, a child of a Kindertransport refugee, created together with Mark Harris a brilliant, Academy Award-winning film entitled *Into the Arms of Strangers,* which told the story of the Kindertransport through the narration of its refugee children. The film was powerful and poignant. I experienced the film on two levels: as the child that I used to be and as the parent I had since become. As a child, separation from a parent is a nightmare, often one's worst fear. To hear the children describe their moment of parting was painful. There were no easy stories, no simple tales. Children who intellectually understood what their parents had done – their love for their children was so deep that to enable them to live they were willing to give them away – still felt that they had been abandoned and could not *emotionally* forgive their parents for leaving them. Those whose parents did not survive the Holocaust felt that abandonment keenly; they were abandoned forever.

And those whose parents had survived and were reunited with them felt a deep sense of estrangement. They had left home, often as very young children, and saw their parents again seven or eight years later. They were different and their parents were different, often diminished and haunted by the *Shoah*[1]. They experienced each other as strangers, desperately needing each other but equally desperately unable to express and to fulfill those needs.

As a parent, when I saw the film, I was shattered. I had been holding my then young son in my arms and could not imagine letting go, could not fathom what love it took and what discernment it required to understand the dire circumstances in Germany and the

---

1. *Shoah* is the Hebrew word for Holocaust.

lack of realistic alternatives so that the ultimate act of love was to give away your child, never knowing if you would see him or her again.

Still later, I worked with Steven Karras on his marvelous film *About Face* and the book that followed, *The Enemy I Knew,* the story of German-Jewish refugees who fought against Nazi Germany in the Allied armies' advanced combat units and intelligence, and worked as army interpreters and as officials in the occupation of Germany. These boys and girls left Germany as refugees and returned victorious, as men and women tested by battle and honored by being commissioned officers, to see their former neighbors and friends, their former homeland. It was a poignant and proud story different in content and tone from *Into the Arms of Strangers*.

And still later my friend Mona Golabeck, herself the daughter of a Kindertransport refugee child, Lisa Jura, invited me to see her one-woman show on her mother's experience, *The Pianist of Willesden Lane*. Willesden Lane was one of the homes that housed these refugee children. An oppressive headmistress made Lisa Jura's experience even more difficult. Music was her salvation. What Lisa was given by her mother was music, and what kept her alive, productive and creative despite all the losses she underwent as a child, was the music she took from home. Now her daughter was transforming her story in a masterful one-woman performance. Grandmother to daughter and to granddaughter – and indeed to great-granddaughter – the music was what endured. It could be and would be played everywhere and could guard the soul from the devastation that was shattering.

And the very week I sat down to read this book I saw *Nicky's Family*, a new film by Matej Mináč and Patrik Pass, on Sir Nicholas Winton's efforts as a young man to save Czechoslovakian children and bring them to England. So as I sat down to read *Memories That Won't Go Away: A Tribute to the Children of the Kindertransport,* I was joined by my own memories that would not go away and impressed by Michele M. Gold's clear prose and Gabriella Y. Karin's gentle illustrations. The book tells the stories of these refugee children, some in depth and some rather lightly, but story builds on story until one experiences the largest of all stories. The oppression of Jews in Germany and later in German-occupied Austria and German-occupied Czechoslovakia was such that the only safe course was for parents to send those beloved children away, not knowing where they would go, who would raise them and what would become of them. Their act of love and selflessness enabled their children to survive; some lived comfortably and were raised lovingly, and some were not. Survival is no guarantee of the quality of life but merely of life itself.

As we read this book, we are confronted with a paradox not of that world but of the world in which we live. In order to raise wholesome and secure children, we must tell them in words, in silence and in deeds two essential things: the world is safe and we are here to protect you.

Neither is genuinely true, as parents of Newtown learned when they sent their children to school one morning and never saw them alive again, even in a comfortable quasi-rural town in affluent Connecticut. And still we must become, as Abraham Joshua Heschel, the great 20th century Jewish sage, suggested, 'optimists against our better judgment.' We must tell our children that because of life's precariousness, they are ever more precious and while we may not always succeed and while it may not always be in our capacity to succeed, we are there.

With the offer of one's presence, there is a sense of an answer. Without it, there is a void, emptiness.

Gold and Karin have paid their tribute to these children and to the adults they have become. Our tribute to them must be to read this work and confront their world. It should inspire awe but also gratitude for the gifts we have been given, for the freedom and security we enjoy.

FOREWORD

Inspiration for Good Deeds
By Matej Mináč
Czech Filmmaker

According to the ancient wisdoms of Kabbalah, many worlds exist and, it is said, we live in the lowest of them all – the material world. A chain of good deeds connects us to a better world with rich experiences, and bettering ourselves will lead to a more fulfilling life.

Any good deed counts; our whole existence and purpose depend on the actions and goodwill of each of us. We need to wake up our young generation from their inertia, from the cacophony of noise, of entertainment, videogames and television. It is our responsibility and duty to introduce to young people the world beyond them, to teach about what happened in the past, to motivate them to help and care about all the people of the future.

But how can we influence the minds of young people? How can we persuade them that the issue of good deeds is of paramount importance? When we look at history, we see that from the beginning of time we can make a difference through telling powerful stories. People always needed inspiring stories with the endless fight between good and evil. Old legends, Greek Tragedies and the Bible were all the 'university of the people' in ancient times.

I myself had the greatest privilege to work on the Kindertransport films about the 669 Czechoslovakian children who were rescued from the hands of the Nazis by the English humanitarian Sir Nicholas Winton at the outbreak of World War II. In May 2014 he celebrated his 105th birthday.

Sir Nicholas was silent about his brave deeds for fifty years; not even his wife knew.

Because of his heroic efforts in 1939, just before the outbreak of World War II, he now has the largest family in the world. It consists of the rescued children and their families who number around 6000 people. But 'Nicky', as we all call him today, has a much bigger family. There are thousands of students in many countries who are deeply moved by his acts of kindness. They say: 'If such a twenty-nine-year-old guy could so simply have saved so many lives, why can't we do something ourselves?' And they really are inspired to do good deeds. They help the elderly, handicapped and refugees, and children at risk in Africa and Cambodia.

I strongly feel that the efforts of these young people will be significantly strengthened by the book *Memories That Won't Go Away*, written by Michele M. Gold and illustrated by Gabriella Y. Karin. Seeing this unique artistic Kindertransport project, I was overwhelmed by its simplicity, beauty, playfulness and direct inspiration for students, children and their parents all over the world. They will learn from the book, from its images and its captivating stories, how more than seventy years ago parents and children enjoyed a great life together until the moment that hatred, anti-Semitism and violence started to rule in Germany in the 1930s.

Parents had to make the most difficult decision of their lives: to let their children go to safety to England, or not? Would they have the strength at the train station to say a last farewell to their children and maybe never see them again? This book is a powerful testimony of great love and great sacrifice, and of the enormous risk that was taken to save these children.

These stories will resonate in our hearts forever. The presentations and documented history in this book will have an immense impact on young people and will guide them to do something good for others.

'Children are our Future'

INTRODUCTION

By Michele M. Gold

My mother lost her brave fight with cancer on October 4, 2008. The death of a parent is a profoundly life-changing experience. When my mother died, a little of me died with her. My mother was the essence of all that is good, with a determination and inner strength that inspired us all. She was a true *Eshet Chayil* (a woman of valor). As my niece Deborah said with such emotion and dignity at my mother's funeral: 'With all that she encountered in her young life, she never reflected back on the cruel horrors that had surrounded her; she was the most positive person and just so grateful to have been given the chance of a good life.'

My mother rarely allowed herself to think about her past; it was too painful for her. For her, there were memories that would never go away. Over the years, my husband Larry and I were fortunate enough to have my mother staying with us in Los Angeles to escape the cold winter months in London. It was during these visits that my mother and I had our deepest conversations, allowing her to talk about her past.

It was in the depth of my grieving and sadness that I found a measure of comfort when I started working with Gabriella Karin at the Los Angeles Museum of the Holocaust. Gabriella is a Holocaust survivor and an artist, who with insight and creativity decided to express the plight and struggle of the *kinder* by creating a ceramic train sculpture as a tribute to the child survivors that were saved by the Kindertransports. I collected photos and brief biographies of hundreds of *kinder*, the idea being that a photo of every *kind* would carefully be inserted into each of the carved-out windows of the ceramic trains.

On February 6, 2011, the exhibition 'A Tribute to the Children of the Kindertransports' opened at the Los Angeles Museum of the Holocaust. Gabriella and I believe it was very successful. Schools, colleges and universities sent their students and we captured their imaginations as they crowded around the exhibit, eager and anxious to learn as much as they could about how approximately 10,000 children were saved by the Kindertransports. They were deeply affected seeing

1

all the young, apprehensive and hopeful faces in each of the carriages.

After the success of the exhibition, I reflected more deeply on my mother's journey to safety on a Kindertransport out of Leipzig, Germany, and the terrible fate of my natural grandparents. I was inspired to document more fully the stories of the actual people symbolized in Gabriella's train sculptures, to create this keepsake for our future generations. My constant motivation has been my mother: what a wonderful way to honor her. I know this is something she would have very much wanted me to do because we talked about her past frequently and deeply during her illness.

I was further motivated because I felt having been born and grown up in the UK, where so many of these children arrived, and with my background, I could make a contribution and turn this into an educational project, sharing with the public the story of the Kindertransport as an integral part of the Holocaust.

In the course of compiling this book, I researched the stories of hundreds of *kinder* and collected photos and artifacts from all over the world. I contacted organizations, museums, synagogues and individuals to gather their oral and written histories, pictures and documents. The response was immediate. The Kindertransport Association (KTA) in New York and the Association of Jewish Refugees (AJR) in the UK printed my articles in their *KinderLink* publication. The Winton Train Office in Prague also sent out press releases to their membership. The many organizations and newspaper publications that were contacted all responded by including press releases in their newsletters. The Belsize Square Synagogue in London, which has a very large membership of *kinder,* sent out a bulletin in its newsletters and very soon I was receiving photos and stories and numerous transcripts from all over the world from *kinder* entrusting me to use and tell the story of their most private memories.

Since 2007, I have been a volunteer docent educator at the Los Angeles Museum of the Holocaust. This is a museum that I am passionate about. Founded in 1961 by a group of Holocaust survivors, it is the oldest Holocaust museum in the United States. In October 2010 the museum moved to its permanent home in Pan Pacific Park, Los Angeles, California. Many of the artifacts that are exhibited are from survivors who have donated some of their most personal memories to the museum. I am fortunate enough to be able contribute to its mission to 'educate and commemorate', an experience that I find tremendously rewarding and gratifying.

Writing this book about the Kindertransport children and documenting the stories of the real people affected has been a life-changing journey for me. It is my deepest hope that it will keep this very important part of our history alive and that people will recognize names and find each other.

My special thanks goes to each and every one of the *kinder* who offered their photographs and their stories, some of which I have recorded in this book.

Throughout this book I use the German words '*kind*' and '*kinder*' to mean '*child*' and '*children*' respectively. This is how many of the survivors of the Kindertransports still refer to themselves after more than seventy years.

My Wartime Memories
By Gabriella Y. Karin

I was born to loving parents and I had an adoring grandmother who lived with us. The world seemed to be a perfect place until, one day, the walls of secure living came crashing down. I was eight years old when Kristallnacht happened. I remember my family sitting together, trying to comprehend how something so horrible could happen and if it would affect us all as well. My father, Arpád Földeš, did not want to believe that this horrendous event had actually occurred.

My mother, Šari Földešová (née Kulka), wanted to leave the country, believing the awful news, afraid that it would happen in Czechoslovakia. She immediately joined the underground, secretly obtaining advance police round-up lists and helping any way she could. I joined her as a night decoy so she could alert those who were scheduled to be picked up. Although I do not remember hearing about the Kindertransport program, I clearly recall my parents hiring an English teacher for me, in hindsight, with a desire to send me to England where the quotas were only for children. I never made it to England, but remained in hiding in Czechoslovakia to suffer the horrors of World War II.

My traumatic memories will never leave me. It is impossible to describe the horror, pain, grief and utter hopelessness we felt during World War II and the Holocaust. I was hidden in a convent for three years with false papers, acting as though I was just another Christian girl among the rest. The nuns were very kind to me but I constantly worried and was fearful about my parents' well-being. I secretly cried myself to sleep every night with worry. Finally, when my mother visited me at the convent and saw my skinny face and glossy eyes, she decided that I would stay in the convent only during

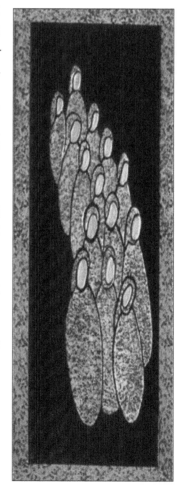

'The Nuns'

school hours and return to her at night. This saved my life in the long run, because when the Germans occupied Slovakia, I went into hiding together with my parents. For nine months, a Righteous Among the Nations, Karol Blanar (*left*), hid my aunt, my parents, two uncles, two friends of my parents and me. From my hiding place, I watched as the two Jewish sisters who had been hiding in the convent with me tried to escape and were caught, never to be seen again.

I now express my thoughts and memories through my artwork. I am forever amazed and impressed with the generosity of people who, by risking their own lives, helped to save so many Jewish people.

Creating a ceramic sculpture as a tribute to the children that were saved by the Kindertransports has been a deeply reflective experience for me. I have learned so much about the *kinder* and their families. I often imagine how these children grew up and continued with their own lives.

'Hidden in the Shadows of Death'

I will forever be grateful to Michele Gold, whose dedication and passion have allowed me to express my creativity fully in this book.

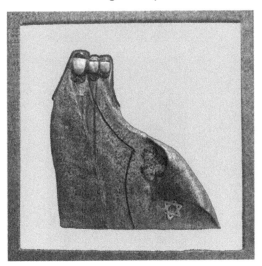

'The Rescuers'

Kristallnacht
November 9–10, 1938 • The Turning Point

Life became increasingly restrictive and difficult for the Jews of Germany after Hitler came to power in 1933. They felt restrictions and persecution in every area of their lives: in schools, shops, offices and in some cities, where signs were displayed saying: 'Jews not welcome.' Along with the discrimination, there were forced mass deportations of foreign Jews from Germany. In October 1938, 17,000 Jews with Polish citizenship, many of whom had been living in Germany for years, were arrested and deported to Poland. They were refused entry, however, and were interned in refugee camps on the German-Polish border.

Herschel Grynszpan (*left*), a seventeen-year-old Jewish man who was living in Paris, found out that his Polish-born parents were among those arrested and held in a camp on the border. Devastated at his parents' plight, and wanting to draw worldwide attention to what was happening, he stormed the German Embassy in Paris on November 7, 1938, and shot Ernst vom Rath (*right*), a diplomatic official. Vom Rath died of his wounds two days later.

The assassination provided Joseph Goebbels (*below right*), Hitler's propaganda minister, with the perfect excuse to orchestrate brutal attacks against the Jews. On November 9 he gave a rousing speech to Nazi party leaders in the Munich *Altes Rathaus* (Old Town Hall) indicating that any 'spontaneous' attacks on Jewish stores, community centers and synagogues by Germans deciding to take the law into their own hands would not be repressed.

During the night and the following day

of November 9-10, mobs freely attacked Jews throughout Germany and in recently annexed Austria and the Sudetenland region of Czechoslovakia. Over a thousand synagogues were severely damaged and hundreds were set on fire. Jewish cemeteries were desecrated and homes were ransacked. Thousands of Jews were arrested and sent to concentration camps. Sledgehammers were used to smash the windows of Jewish buildings and shop fronts and some were totally demolished. The streets were left covered in broken glass after the pogrom, which is why it became known as *Kristallnacht* – the Night of the Broken Glass.

Kristallnacht was a terrifying foretaste of the horrors and darkness of the Final Solution that lay ahead for the Jews of Europe. It was a pivotal event that shocked people outside of Germany into some action to help the Jews. On November 15, 1938, British Jewish and Quaker leaders met Neville Chamberlain, the British prime minister, and appealed to him to allow unaccompanied Jewish children into Britain, thus setting in motion the rescue mission that would become known as the Kindertransport.

The venue for Joseph Goebbel's speech on November 9, 1938
(known as the prelude to Kristallnacht)

Photo credits: Ernst Vom Rath – United States Holocaust Memorial Museum, courtesy of Oesterreichische National Bibliothek • Joseph Goebbels – Bundesarchiv, Bild 102-17049 / Foto: George Pahl / Licence CC-BY-SA 3.0 • Herschel Grynszpan – Courtesy of United States Holocaust Memorial Museum

Kindertransport History
and
Frequently Asked Questions

Life Before and After the Holocaust

Before the Holocaust there were about sixteen million Jewish people worldwide of whom it is estimated about nine million lived in Europe. The most quoted figure for the total number of Jews that perished in extermination and concentration camps and mass open-air shootings during the Holocaust is approximately six million. This figure includes those that died in ghettos due to overcrowding, unsanitary conditions, typhus and malnutrition.

After liberation the death toll continued to rise. Many died in displacement camps from the after-effects of malnutrition. The Holocaust wiped out about two-thirds of the European Jewish population, or one-third of the world Jewish population.

What is a Holocaust Survivor?

A Holocaust survivor is anyone who survived the systematic, state-organized policy of extermination of European Jewry perpetrated by Nazi Germany and its allies and collaborators. Any individual, Jewish or non-Jewish, who was persecuted, displaced and/or discriminated against due to the racial, religious, ethnic, social and political policies of the Nazis and survived, is a Holocaust survivor. The Kindertransport children are child Holocaust survivors.

What was the Kindertransport?

The Kindertransport – children's transport – was a rescue mission that was hurriedly put together as a response to the events that took place on November 9 and 10, 1938, called Kristallnacht (Night of the Broken Glass). The Kindertransport took children to safety in sealed trains. Approximately 10,000 children were rescued on the Kindertransport from December 1, 1938, to September 1, 1939, just before the outbreak of World War II, which marked the end of this program.

How was the Kindertransport Formed?

After Kristallnacht and the reports of statewide terror, it was clear that all Jews faced immediate danger. A visionary plan to rescue children was formulated by the Central British Fund for German Jewry (established in 1933 and now known as World Jewish Relief) together with dedicated volunteers, Christians, Quakers and refugee agencies who all came together to help fund the operation now known as the Kindertransport. Great Britain waived immigration requirements so as to allow the entry of unaccompanied children ranging from infants up to the age of seventeen, without passports or visas, with no restrictions. The only condition put upon these children was that every child would have a guarantee of fifty pounds sterling so they wouldn't be a burden to the state. It was expected that the children would stay in the country only temporarily and would eventually return home. However, very few children were ever reunited with their families.

The Kindertransport Journey

On December 1, 1938, the first Kindertransport left from Berlin with 200 children travelling together, but alone. Soon children were leaving from Germany, Austria, Poland and Czechoslovakia and arriving in the UK. Some of them stayed in hostels; most of the younger ones were sent to live with foster families. Only a few children had pre-arranged sponsors waiting for them. No *kinder* were accompanied by their parents; a few were babies carried by older children. The experience for them all was traumatic. There were heartbreaking scenes when siblings were separated. For the very young, it was confusing. They did not understand why they were being separated from their parents. The experience for the parents was harrowing beyond our imaginations. Many of the parents who sent their children to safety on the Kindertransports perished in the Holocaust.

Some of the Key Figures in the Rescue Operation

Many heroic men and women helped organize the departure of the trains from Germany, Austria, Czechoslovakia and Poland. Following an appeal from Stanley Baldwin, a former British prime minister, and others, Trevor Chadwick went to Prague and brought back two Jewish boys to the school in Dorset, in southwest England, where he was a teacher.

He returned to Prague and met with Doreen Warriner, who was the senior representative there of the British Committee for Refugees. Her main concern initially was with political refugees from the Sudetenland following the Nazi invasion. Nicholas Winton arrived in Prague at the request of Martin Blake, a friend of his, who in December 1938 was there visiting Doreen Warriner. When Winton saw for himself the refugee camps and the dire situation facing all Jewish people, especially the children, he decided to set up his own rescue mission from the hotel in Wenceslas Square where he was staying. He started interviewing parents and before long, they were lining up to meet him, begging him to include their children on his lists and take them to England.

Winton remained in Prague for about two weeks, returning to London with a suitcase full of photos of children and lists of their names. He began to search for families willing to accept Jewish children. He went back to work, but at the end of each day he devoted his time to his rescue mission. He formed an organization that consisted of himself, his mother, his secretary and a few volunteers. He placed advertisements in the newspapers looking for British families willing to take in these children. He wrote to people throughout Britain and tried to match each child with the right foster family. He persuaded the Home Office to let the children into the country, and worked very closely with the officials who issued the entry permits.

Winton needed someone to run his operation at the Prague end, and Trevor Chadwick offered to perform this role, returning in February and remaining there until June, some three months after the Nazi invasion in March 1939. Chadwick worked tirelessly, making the arrangements, organizing the trains, interviewing the families and sending Winton the details of the individual children. Meanwhile, Doreen Warriner had been continuing her separate work with other refugees until April, when she was forced to leave because her life was in danger. Beatrice Wellington from Vancouver, Canada, took over her work.

These courageous people remained in Prague, putting themselves in danger, to enable the children to leave. Between them, the rescuers ensured the survival of several thousand refugees. *For more information about Sir Nicholas Winton see page 71 and Trevor Chadwick see page 150.*

What Happened to the Children After the War?

The majority of the children who lost their families stayed in Great Britain and made their lives there. Many who had surviving family members scattered around the world joined them. Some children went to the United States, Canada or Australia, and many went to Israel. The end of the war brought to light the terrible reality that most of these children's parents had not survived. Out of the 10,000 rescued children, about 90% lost their parents. Although these children were fortunate to survive the Holocaust, many lived with a terrible guilt that they had survived and a deep grief that stayed with them their entire lives.

Why was the Kindertransport so Important?

The 10,000 brave young survivors were small in number compared to the some 1.5 million children who perished in the Holocaust. But for these child refugees, leaving home on the Kindertransport – traumatic though it was – meant the difference between life and death.

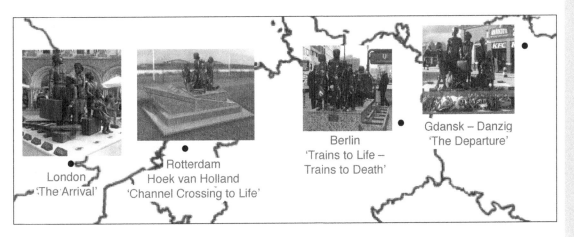

London 'The Arrival'

Rotterdam Hoek van Holland 'Channel Crossing to Life'

Berlin 'Trains to Life – Trains to Death'

Gdansk – Danzig 'The Departure'

Kindertransport sculptures by Frank Meisler

IMAGINE...
It Wasn't Happily Ever After
for All the *Kinder*

IMAGINE if you can, how a child would feel being told they were going to have to leave their parents and family, sometimes in a great hurry, with little or no time for any preparation, to travel alone to a foreign country and learn a new language. Even in normal situations some children fear being separated from their parents – and these were exceptional circumstances. I myself, remember as a child loathing my parents going out for fear that they may not return home again and I would be left alone. A child needs to feel protected and loved by a parent, and constantly reassured of any doubts and insecurities.

IMAGINE the parents, who had to suppress their feelings outwardly, but inside they ached having to tell their child that they would have to go away, far away, to a new country and learn a foreign language, be polite and be very well behaved until they could all be reunited again. It was a heartbreaking, traumatic experience for the parent who felt helpless, in a hopeless situation because they knew it was unlikely that they would ever see their child again once the train left the station.

IMAGINE children torn from their families, most never seeing their parents again, arriving in England, many not knowing where they were going. Some families took one or two children. Some selected an older child for the purposes of 'domestic help' or to work in a farm or to do household chores. In some cases, children, all alone, went to hostels, orphanages and other institutions, most speaking very little English.

IMAGINE how frightening it was for the children, some so young they didn't understand why they had been separated from their loving families and now they were finding themselves being cared for by strangers who did not speak the same language or eat the same foods. Imagine what it would feel like to be in a strange country, placed in the care of people with different customs and a different set of values.

All this made communication so very difficult. The children's daily routines were, in an instant, dramatically changed. Some of the children came from deeply devout and observant families. Sometimes, there was little sensitivity regarding their cultural and religious needs.

IMAGINE how young children would express themselves if they needed to go to the bathroom or make themselves understood if they were hungry or sick – very young children could well have been totally disorientated and frightened.

IMAGINE how hard it was for the children who were old enough to understand why they had been separated from their parents and families. They had to cope with the fear and the awareness of what their loved ones were possibly facing. Most clung to the hope that eventually they would be reunited with their parents and families. Few ever were.

IMAGINE what it was like for some of these children who lived with deep grief and guilt and were tormented for the rest of their lives.

Most children had lived happy childhood years, mostly unaffected by the political and economic crisis and until 1933 experienced little or no anti-Semitism.

Research, memoirs and interviews have revealed that the experiences for the *kinder* were so complicated – and in some instances so painful – but for all their individual encounters, they remain unequivocally grateful to the nation that saved them. Many of the children of the Kindertransports did not consider themselves as 'survivors'. Perhaps if they had, they would have had a chance to somehow heal a little and it would not have remained so 'raw' for most of their lives.

BUT with all that the *kinder* experienced, they knew that life must go on because this is the way of the world. But they will never forget what happened during the Holocaust. In the words of the former Chief Rabbi of Britain and the Commonwealth, Lord Sacks: 'We can't change the past, but each of us, by challenging prejudice and intolerance, can help change the future.'

RITA BERWALD (NÉE RIMALOWER-NETTLER)

My mother was born in Leipzig, Germany, on February 11, 1924. She left on a Kindertransport in March 1939. This is my mother's story, the unabbreviated version as she wrote it in her own words in early 1992.

– Michele Gold

Memories That Won't Go Away
By Rita Berwald

The end of my childhood was quickly realized one day after I had finished my homework with Edith, my best friend. We had studied and tested each other for the end-of-term exams, and after feeling reasonably ready for the big day, I left Edith for home.

Walking quickly and before I had a chance to cross the street, I saw it… two young men in their early twenties, dressed in Hitler's uniform, with brown shirts and swastika armbands, complete with jackboots, were handing out leaflets. My heart was pounding as I heard the sharp command, 'Halt!' Knowing that I must not flinch, I looked straight into the uniformed man's eyes.

'You must salute *Heil Hitler* when passing the Torch!' he said. Do it at once, I was told.

'I am not allowed to salute,' I responded. 'I am Jewish.'

He stared at me and then by the grace of the Almighty I was ordered to go home. I ran home and was greeted at the door by my eldest brother with whom I shared the story, shaking and crying.

This was the first realization of what Hitler's reign of terror really meant. It meant the end of my childhood. I was fourteen years old.

My eldest brother Harry had seen there was no future for him in Germany and decided to make his way to Holland where my uncle lived; my uncle agreed to give Harry money to help him to reach South America.

The loan was necessary as the Hitler regime restricted Jewish emigrants from taking more than a few marks out of Germany.

My father, honest to a fault, constantly worried about reimbursing my uncle.

At that time, one was still able to leave the country to go on holiday. The allowance of currency per person per year, although far from generous, if carefully used, might help pay the debt. A plan was devised for my father and me to travel to Scheveningen, a seaside resort outside The Hague and not far from Amsterdam, where we would stay at a modest but clean hotel and spend as little money as possible. After a week or so, my father was to return to Germany and my brother Peter, who was nineteen years old, would join me in Amsterdam in order for him to take his holiday allowance out of the country, and so the money saved with this holiday allowance would settle what we owed my uncle.

My mother managed to add to this by making a trip to Switzerland, where she stayed with her sister for a short time. The debt was paid.

Perhaps I was too young to realize the terrible events that were unfolding, and so I enjoyed the holiday. Exploring the beach, I met a girl of my own age and we exchanged names – hers was Doris. She told me she was Scottish – on holiday with her parents, her sister Joyce and her two brothers, Raymond and Merton.

My father and Doris's parents met and talked a great deal before my father left to return to Germany. To me, those days were happy and

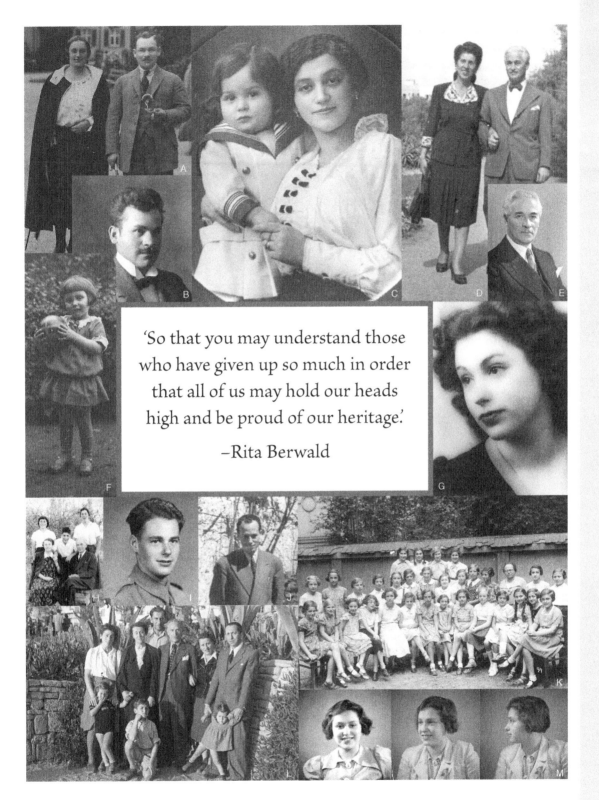

'So that you may understand those who have given up so much in order that all of us may hold our heads high and be proud of our heritage.'

–Rita Berwald

A: Marie & Febus Rimalower B: Febus Rimalower C: Harry & Marie Rimalower
D: Annie & Fred Nettler E: Fred Nettler F: Rita Rimalower-Nettler G: Rita
H: Family Photo I: Peter Rodney (who changed his name when he arrived in the UK
from Wolfgang Rimalower) J: Harry Rimalower K: Rita's School Year Photo – Leipzig
L: Family gathering M: Rita

A: Rita Nettler B: Doris Nettler C: Raymond Nettler D: Rita & Doris Nettler
E: Joyce Nettler F: Annie Nettler G: Fred, Annie, Joyce & Rita Nettler H: Fred Nettler

carefree – I learned later that they had begged my father not to go back. Soon our holiday ended. It was time to go our separate ways: Doris and her family to Glasgow, and my brother and me to Leipzig. We promised to write and indeed we did, regularly.

In the meantime, the situation in Germany grew worse and more dangerous. Peter was in a road accident that damaged the car of a high-ranking SS Officer and was packed off in a great hurry that same evening to my aunt in Switzerland. My parents were heartbroken. They were powerless to help my brothers further, and just prayed for them to be safe and anxiously waited for news of them.

Very soon after this incident was Kristallnacht, November 9-10, 1938. The telephone rang in the middle of the night and my father was forced to go to his business premises to clear up the shattered glass and clean off the obscenities that had been painted all over the frontage of his building. I was left alone as my parents rushed off. It took them the rest of the night to clean up the damage. No one was allowed to help them. When they finally came home, it was daylight. They looked worn out and downtrodden. My heart sank. This was the end of my father's business, a small store on two floors where people could buy beautiful table and bed linens. It was now closed. A few days later, an official came and sealed off the doors, froze all the assets including my father's bank accounts, business and private, dismissed all the staff and decided on a small allowance, which was to be released to my father out of his now state-controlled account in order that he could buy a little food and very bare necessities. Worse was to come.

I continued attending school – a Jewish school. One day, in the middle of a lesson, my teacher was called out of the classroom. When she returned, her face was ashen. She read out a number of names and told those children to put their coats on and leave. Then, with tears streaming down her face, she told the rest of the children who had not been named to go home quickly and as quietly as possible.

I saw lots of children of various ages being herded into great trucks by uniformed men in black. There were adults too, and they were crying, and I ran all the way home. It was not too far from my school. My mother was there to greet me and I began to cry. I cried for the horror I had just seen on the teachers' faces; I cried for all the frightened children who did not know what was happening to them. I cried for my parents, who, for the very first time ever, could not make everything alright for me, and I cried because my world was shattered.

My school was closed; no more school – no more friends. No one ventured out of their houses. Then one morning they arrived. Men, swarms of men, armed with enormous sticks, charging into Jewish homes beating up men, women and children, breaking and destroying everything in sight.

My parents had again been ordered to my father's business where more damage had deliberately been inflicted. Somehow they managed to contact me to tell me to leave the house at once and meet them at a special place. I was terrified. I walked out of my home straight into a mob of perhaps twenty men all wielding great sticks, spitting and shouting obscenities to me, and again, by the grace of the Almighty, I was allowed to walk away and continue walking until I reached the hiding place where my parents and I stayed with relatives.

We could not return home for some time, so we went into hiding with relatives who took us in. Very soon after this, a letter arrived from Glasgow from the family that my parents, brother and I met while holidaying in Holland, inviting me to join them in Glasgow. Fred and Annie Nettler promised to treat and love me as their own for as long as I needed to live there. So it was decided by my mother and father that they would send me away to safety. After many applications, permission was given for me to leave Germany.

I always remembered how my parents tried so hard to see to it that I was well dressed and not short of anything. I was old enough to know that they must have denied themselves a great deal. I remember my case being packed and the plans we made for when my parents would join me in Great Britain. I remember the night before I was to leave: I was preparing for bed and having my bath when my mother knocked on the door and came in. She sat on the edge of the tub and suddenly she said, trying to explain, 'We are sending you away, only, because you know it is easier for us to move about, if the need arose, knowing you are safe.' Then she put her arms around me and held me close.

The day I left on the Kindertransport, my mother, who normally was so emotional, hugged and kissed me and smiled and my father, always so strong, hugged and held me very tight. It was so hard to be strong and not cry. I knew they could not have endured it. So I fought back the tears, but could not stop the ache in my heart. I boarded the train and that was the last time I ever saw them. My brave, brave parents. I am absolutely certain that they knew what was to be. It was many years later that I fully understood what our parting had cost them.

The journey to England was exciting. It dulled the pain. So much going on and so much to see. There were many young children who looked so lost. Then there were some nearer my age who did not know where they were going and did not know what was in store for them.

We arrived in London and a friend of the Nettlers met me and put me on the Edinburgh Express. He was very kind and he asked the steward on the train to look after me. When the train pulled out of the station, I felt so alone. I remember how attentive the steward was. He kept asking me if he could bring me anything and he reappeared with a plate of assorted biscuits. I won't ever forget his kindness.

I arrived in Edinburgh at about 11:30pm on March 3, 1939, and was met by Fred Nettler. We traveled the final lap of the journey by car. When we arrived at my new home in Glasgow, I was welcomed by Annie Nettler.

It was very late by then and before going to bed it was decided that I would call my hosts 'Uncle and Aunt'. They so wanted me to be part of the family. The next morning I had a great welcome from all the family and that great warmth and love between us has always remained.

The war broke out in September 1939 and shortly after that there was no more news from my parents. A friend of the family with whom I lived had traced them and made sure they knew I was safe and well. My parents had managed to escape over the Polish border and that was the last I ever heard from them.

I began a new life. I went to school and learned to live without fear. I was one of the lucky ones. My brother Peter finally gained entry into Great Britain. He joined the army and spent the war years in the Pioneer Corps. My adopted family became mother, father, sisters and brothers to me. My own parents have forever stayed in my heart.

Thirty-four years later my elder brother Harry came on a visit from Los Angeles, where he had settled with his family. We got on wonderfully well and spent precious time together getting to know each other again. The long years of separation fell away. He died of cancer eighteen months after his visit. It was such a devastating loss. I had only just found my big brother again.

Peter, my other natural brother, lives in Glasgow with his wife Joan, son Philip and daughter Jackie. His wife and family have given him much joy. He, like so many survivors of the Holocaust, is very much affected by what happened in his life.

I got married and had two wonderful children – Melvin and Michele – who grew up straight and true and are a great source of happiness to me. My son married Sharman, who became like another daughter, and they have a lovely little girl, Deborah, who is the darling of all the family. And now Michele, my daughter, is getting married to Larry, a fine, caring man, who already occupies a place deep in my heart, and this is my time for reflection.

Courtesy of Rita's children and grandchildren who are so inspired by her – Michele and Larry, Melvin and Sharman, Deborah and her husband Alex, and Leah (Rita's younger granddaughter born shortly after she wrote her story).

EDWARD BEHRENDT

Edward 'Eddy' Behrendt was born in Danzig, Germany in January 1930. Eddy was just nine years old when he left Danzig on a Kindertransport to England. He stayed in England until 1946, and after a brief stay in Israel (then Palestine), came to America to be with his father who had survived the Holocaust and immigrated to New York.

In 1989 Eddy founded and became the first president of the Kindertransport Association (KTA). He saw the Kindertransport as a part of Holocaust history that had not been fully explored. With the help of the Simon Wiesenthal Center, the KTA, under Eddy's guidance and dedication, began searching for the Kindertransport children who had come to the United States. After an enormous amount of work, the KTA brought over 500 *kinder* and family members together for a very emotional reunion.

After his retirement, Eddy and his wife moved to the Phoenix/Scottsdale area where he served on the Board of the Phoenix Holocaust

Survivors Association. In later years, he and his wife Sarah formed another organization to provide education for all students from the age of ten to college-level regarding World War II and the atrocities millions were forced to endure. The organization, based in Eugene, Oregon, where they had moved in 1995, was called 'Reach and Teach'. For four years he and his wife taught Holocaust history and related events to schoolchildren throughout Oregon.

Courtesy of the Kindertransport Association: www.kindertransport.org

Danzig, Germany 1930

LILLIAN LICHTMAN (NÉE KRAMER)

Shortly after Kristallnacht, Lillian and her brother Walter joined a group that took them to Brussels, Belgium, where they were placed with different families. A year later, they went to England and boarded the *Lancastria* to New York, where they were reunited with their parents.

Courtesy of Lillian Kramer-Lichtman, Los Angeles, California, USA

Train 2

ADI KIMMELFELD

HORST CAHN

HORST WOLFF

SALI OBERNICKER

PIERRE MARCUSE

Jewish refugee boys Adi Kimmelfeld, Horst Cahn, Horst Wolff, Sali Obemicker and Pierre Marcuse came to France on a Kindertransport from Germany.

ADI KIMMELFELD

These young boys were amongst a group of German-Jewish refugee children that were taken to a chateau at Quincy-sous-Senart (about seventeen miles southeast of Paris). The chateau belonged to the Count Hubert de Monbrison before World War II. He and his wife Princess Irena Paley used the chateau to house refugee girls. In 1939 the count was approached by his

HORST CAHN

HORST WOLFF

SALI OBERNICKER

PIERRE MARCUSE

children's Jewish physician, who was a member of the board of the

Oeuvre de Secours aux Enfants (OSE) children's aid society, and was asked if he would take in a group of forty German refugee children. The count agreed. The Kindertransport of boys arrived on July 4, 1939. The chateau served as a Jewish children's home until September 1940, following the German occupation of France when the chateau was requisitioned by the German army.

The boys were then transferred to other OSE homes.

A chateau at Quincy-sous-Senart

United States Holocaust Memorial Museum, courtesy of Lida Jablonski

Train 3

VERA GISSING (NÉE DIAMANTOVA)

Vera was born in Prague in 1928. Vera and her older sister, Eva Hayman, were both rescued by Nicholas Winton. Vera was almost eleven when she arrived in England on Winton's second Czech Kindertransport.

CHILD A WINTON

She never considered herself to be a Holocaust survivor, but just a young girl who was sent to England until after the war.

Vera lived with foster parents before she joined the school in Wales for Czech refugee children. Throughout the war years, she kept a meticulous diary recording her experiences. After the war she returned to Prague to study and in 1949 moved back to England, where she married and had three children.

Vera enjoyed translating books from Czech into English as a hobby. Later she started writing her own books, mainly for children. In 1988 she wrote *Pearls of Childhood*, the story of a young child growing up in extraordinary times, based on her own wartime

diaries. The book was introduced into schools and colleges and is recognized as an important piece of social history.

Courtesy of Vera Gissing, UK

Vera with her father and sister Eva

Family photo

CHILD SLEEPING WITH A DOLL

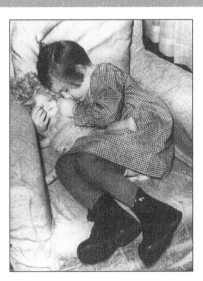

One of the refugee children who had just arrived at Harwich, Essex, on the second Kindertransport, December 1938.

Courtesy of United States Holocaust Memorial Museum

A group of boys from Bratislava prepare to leave for England on a Kindertransport.

Max was born in Bratislava, Czechoslovakia, on March 2, 1921. He had two sisters, Trude and Lilly, and four younger brothers, Kurt, Harry, Josi and Robi.

Even at a young age, Max was deeply interested in stamps. He had no idea of their value but simply wanted as many different stamps from as many different countries as he could find. After Hitler came to power in 1933, life became harder for the Jews in Europe. Max began trading stamps for money and by the time he was fourteen, he was paying his own school fees. In 1936 he went to Vienna to study mechanical engineering and came home to Bratislava at the weekends. In March 1938 Germany annexed Austria and immediately anti-Semitism became rampant. Max could no longer continue his studies in Vienna, so he returned home. As the oldest of seven children, it became his responsibility to be the main provider for his family through his stamp dealing. The family depended on him, so he had no choice but to start trading full-time. In May 1939 his family was torn apart when two of Max's younger brothers, Kurt and Harry, went to safety to Britain on the Kindertransport. They were fostered with gentile families. Kurt at that time was aged about eleven and Harry was about ten.

Max continued to operate his business throughout most of World War II. After escaping the final deportation of Czech Jews in late 1944, Max went into hiding until he was discovered in late 1944 and deported to the Sachsenhausen concentration camp, close to Berlin. When the war finally ended, he had survived a death march from Berlin towards Hamburg. He returned to Bratislava and was reunited with his two sisters, Trude and Lilly. He learned that his parents and younger brothers had been taken to Auschwitz.

In 1945 Max reestablished his stamp business in Bratislava, but the communist takeover of Czechoslovakia three years later made it impossible for him to continue. He and his wife, Eva, made their way to Australia. He established himself as a stamp dealer in 1950, opening a shop in Melbourne.

Max went on to become a worldwide authority on stamps and at the time of writing, aged over 90, he is Australia's best-known stamp dealer and has received many honors. In June 1999 he received the Order of Australia in the Queen's Birthday Honors list 'for services to philately, particularly in the promotion of Australian stamp series overseas'.

Max is considered one of the most famous stamp dealers in the world.

Max Stern is the author of two books:
My Stamp on Life and *The Max Factor –*
My Life as a Stamp Dealer
(text extracts taken from the latter).

Group photo courtesy of the United States Holocaust Memorial Museum

Three schoolchildren, who were part of the Kindertransport movement, sitting at a table in their classroom at Bunce Court School. The hostel was home to fifty boys from Germany, Austria and Poland. It was located in the village of Otterden in Kent, England. It was founded by Anna Essinger and two of her sisters in 1926. Anna was generally called *Tante* (Aunt) Anna. She was strict, but the school environment was loving and supportive.

Bunce Court School in Kent, England

United States Holocaust Memorial Museum, courtesy of Bernard Kelly

KINDER GROUP IN SCOTLAND

The Priory, a children's home in Selkirk, Scotland, was one of many homes and hostels that took in refugee children who came on the Kindertransport. The Priory also served as a holiday home for under-privileged children from Edinburgh who had experienced stressful home circumstances.

United States Holocaust Memorial Museum, courtesy of Gunther Abrahamson

31

KINDER GIRLS SEWING AT WHITTINGEHAME

A training farm and school was established on the estate of Viscount Traprain in Whittingehame, in East Lothian, Scotland, to provide shelter for German and Austrian Jewish youngsters who were part of the Kindertransports. Viscount Traprain, the nephew of Lord Balfour, offered his estate to the Edinburgh Jewish Congregation in the winter of 1938-9. One hundred and sixty-nine children, under the supervision of twelve adults, studied agriculture, horticulture

and poultry-keeping. After the war the children were reunited with surviving family members or resettled in Israel. Among those who took an active interest in the Whittingehame shelter was Vera Weizmann, the wife of Chaim Weizmann, a Zionist leader and the first president of the State of Israel.

A group of Jewish girls working in the sewing room at the *Hachshara* agricultural training farm, Whittingehame, East Lothian, Scotland.

United States Holocaust Memorial Museum, courtesy of Fay Cohen Stein

TOMMY (FORMERLY GUNTHER) STRAUSS

Gunther was born in July 1926. He arrived in England alone on a Kindertransport in July 1939 when he was thirteen years old.

Courtesy of Tommy Strauss, Forest Hills, New York, USA

Two nights before Peter's seventh birthday, he and his family were awakened by the sound of breaking glass and yelling as their home in Nuremberg was vandalized. Kristallnacht was just the beginning of the Nazi violence against Jews, and it shaped the rest of Peter's life.

Two months later, on January 5, 1939, Peter left Frankfurt on a Kindertransport and became one of thousands of children who were granted safe refuge in England from Germany. Peter's parents found a sponsor and a few months after his arrival in England, just before the start of World War II, they were able to join him. Peter was among a very small number of children who were reunited with their parents.

A year later, Peter and his family left England for the United States. He went to college to study art. After studying design in an art school, he became a product designer for Philco Corporation, designing home entertainment products. In 1959 Peter joined the Aerospace Division at the Martin Company (now Lockheed Martin) and became head of their human factors group. Soon after, he decided he wanted to become a lawyer and took classes at night. Upon admission to the Bar, he opened his law office in 1966. Peter became an appellate judge at the Colorado Court of Appeals in 1988, where he served until 2003, when he became a senior Judge.

His family persuaded him to write his memoirs, and his book *Getting Here* describes his journey from a seat on a refugee train to a seat on the appellate bench.

Courtesy of Peter Ney, Littleton, Colorado, USA

Castle in Nuremberg, Germany, 1939

Train Four

33

Sigi was born on November 13, 1931, in Königsbach, Germany. Königsbach was a small town in Baden-Baden, located in the Black Forest district. Jews had lived there since the 1600s. Sigi grew up in an Orthodox Jewish home where he lived with his parents, two sisters and a brother. He was the youngest child. They all lived on the top floor of a two-story house and rented out the lower floor to another family.

He remembers with great clarity as a young boy how his father would pick him up so he could reach the *mezuzah* (prayer parchment) on the bedroom doorpost and recite the *Shema Yisrael*[2] prayer. His parents gave him a normal life as best as they could under the conditions they lived in as Jews in Nazi Germany. In 1938 Sigi attended his first year of school and remembers vividly

House in Königsbach where Sigi and his family lived (center right).

how the teacher one day called him to the front of the class and told him to go home. He had no idea why he was being sent home. He was just six years old; too young to understand the urgency of the situation. It was not until years later that he learned it was part of the Nazi policy that Jewish children could no longer attend public schools. It also included universities and colleges.

After this incident, Sigi and one of his sisters went to a Jewish school. He remembers how he always played alone outside his house because no other children would play with him.

Again, he did not understand why until years later.

The memory of Kristallnacht will stay with him forever. The Nazis came to his house that night and were about to enter when the family living downstairs, who were gentiles, told them that they owned the house. It appears that Sigi's parents had sold it to them.

The Nazis were looking for his father, who fortunately did not come home that day as he had gone to the country to visit his mother. Instead of his father, the Nazis took his brother, who was almost

---

2. *Shema Yisrael* – 'Hear, O Israel' prayer recited every morning and night.

seventeen, away to Dachau, where he remained for several weeks. They released him and he was told within the month he must leave the country or he would be arrested and be taken away as a permanent prisoner.

When Sigi's brother returned home in 1939 his hair had been shaved off. Very soon after his return from Dachau, he left for England. When he arrived, he went to Manchester to stay with a cousin. Later, Sigi's eldest sister left for England to join his brother. Three weeks after Kristallnacht, the Kindertransports were established. Sigi received permission to leave Germany on a Kindertransport. His mother packed a suitcase for him based on the list of permitted items. No valuables were allowed to be taken out of the country.

When the day arrived for him to leave, both Sigi's parents came to the railway station. Parents were not allowed on the platform unless the child was being taken to another city to connect with a Kindertransport. Sigi saw his mother outside the station fence. It was the last time he ever saw her.

Top: Königsbacher Synagogue before Kristallnacht. Center and lower: After the destruction.

Hannchen and Jakob Wasserman, Sigi's parents

Sigi and his father boarded the train to Karlsruhe, the city where he would get the connecting train that would take him out of Germany. At the station in Karlsruhe, his father put him on the train where there were many other children travelling to Holland. They said their goodbyes and this was the last time Sigi ever saw his father.

As the train moved slowly out of the station, German soldiers with guns checked all the luggage of the children, who were Sigi's age and younger, to make sure there were no valuables being taken out of the country.

From Holland, they all boarded a ship to cross the English Channel. Sigi arrived at the port of Harwich on England's southeast coast on June 28, 1939.

Courtesy of Sigi Wasserman, Winnipeg, Manitoba, Canada

Train 5

RENEE MOSS (NÉE IRENA ALPERN)

Renee and her family's story is quite unique. They were the only complete family (children together with parents) to arrive in England via a Kindertransport. She and her family lived in Freiburg, Germany. Although her father was born in Berlin, they had Polish citizenship, not German. As a result, in October 1938, her father, together with all Polish Jewish men, was arrested and imprisoned overnight. The following day, all Polish Jews living in Germany had to leave their homes. They spent four months in Zboncyn refugee camp on the borders of Germany and Poland before being contacted by the Kindertransport. Initially, room was found for her three elder siblings on a Kindertransport ship that was sailing from the Polish port of Gdanya. A little later, the authorities accepted Renee – who was a baby of just twenty months – and her parents. Miraculously, they all sailed on the same ship, the SS *Warszawa*.

Renee and her family arriving in England, February 15, 1939. This photo appeared in several British newspapers.

Courtesy of Renee Moss, Netanya, Israel

GERALD FRY (FORMERLY GERHARD FREY)

Gerald was born in 1924 in Hamburg, Germany. He left Hamburg for England on a Kindertransport in July 1939. He was interned there in 1940 and sent to Canada. In 1941, he was released and returned to England. In 1943 he joined the Royal Armoured Corps and served in Europe as a tank commander from D-Day to VE-Day in the Royal Scots Greys. He served for two years as a war-crimes interpreter with the Intelligence Corps as a Warrant Officer and then immigrated to Canada. Gerald's mother perished in Auschwitz.

Gerald returned to London frequently and while he will always remain eternally grateful to the British for saving his life, he decided to make Canada his home and has lived there for the past sixty years. He married a Canadian lady, who sadly died several years ago. He has three children: one lives in Australia, one is a retired CBC director living in Ottawa and the third, who is married to a Canadian diplomat, has been living in Europe for many years. When they first went abroad, he made a deal that each year on his birthday he would visit them wherever they were posted and he did so until 2009. Consequently, he has been to every European country with the exception of Albania. He is immensely proud of his family's achievements.

Courtesy of Gerald Fry, Ottawa, Ontario, Canada

CHILDREN AT WINDERMERE

Group portrait of Jewish refugee girls who came to Britain on a Kindertransport.

United States Holocaust Memorial Museum, Alisa Tennenbaum

Eve was born in Prague on February 23, 1931. She remembers a very happy childhood where she was the center of her universe. Life was full of gaiety, joy, love and excitement. But this was all to fade away when, at age eight, she left Prague on a Kindertransport to England in the early months of 1939.

Eve was too young to contemplate her new surroundings: the different food, language and customs. She couldn't possibly imagine a future that did not include a reunion with her family and often dreamed of how she would feel when they would finally be reunited. Even in 1943, when the precious Red Cross letters stopped arriving and there was no more contact, it was hard for her to comprehend the horrible reality that she would have to face. It wasn't until the end of the war that Eve learned for certain that she would never see her parents or brother again and that they had perished in Auschwitz.

Many years later, Eve learned of the enormity of the Kindertransport program and despite all the grief, she felt so much gratitude. Gratitude to her parents, who made it possible to send her away to safety, and gratitude to Nicholas Winton, when she learned that she was one of 'Nicky's children'. With sheer tenacity and determination, he made it possible for her and 668 other children to escape to England. Gratitude to the British, who welcomed her and accepted her in their homes, and, in particular, gratitude to Miss Minnie Simmonds, who gave her a permanent loving home and encouraged her to take a good path in life.

Nearly two decades after the end of the war, Eve made her first journey back to Prague and was reunited with members of her family who had survived. Since then, both she and her husband have enjoyed frequent family visits. In 2009, the 'Winton train' reunion was organized by the Czechs to re-enact the 1939 Kindertransport journey. It was meticulously planned, with so much compassion and thought. It was a deeply moving and satisfying experience for Eve and she made many new friends whom she values tremendously.

Her biggest support is her husband, who loves her native land and has so much affection for her family and for her past that he even undertook to learn Czech with Eve!

Courtesy of Eve Leadbeater, UK

Train 6

INGE GUREVICH

Inge was born in 1924 in Breslau, Germany. She arrived in England on a Kindertransport from Germany.

Breslau, Germany

Courtesy of Stuart Gurevich, Ottawa, Ontario, Canada

ANNA WHALE

FRANZ WHALE

Anna was born December 17, 1931, in Vienna, where her father served as a judge. He also taught at the university and eventually became judge of the Court of Appeal. Anna's mother worked as an insurance actuary. Her older brother Franz Antony was born August 14, 1929. Following the Nazi *Anschluss*[3] in March 1938, Anna's parents decided to enroll their children on a Kindertransport to England that was organized by the Quakers.

Anna and Franz left on January 10, 1939. Anna went to a convent in Essex and Franz went to Blankton House, established by the Catholic Committee for Refugees from Germany. In 1940 the British army commandeered the home, and Franz was transferred to Stonyhurst College in Lancashire. Anna and Franz visited one another occasionally and spent holidays with an aunt who had immigrated to England from Poland at the start of the war.

Anna and Franz maintained contact with their parents until 1942, when communication suddenly stopped. They heard nothing of their parents for three years, until they received a letter from the Red Cross confirming that both their parents were alive. They were all reunited in 1947 when first their mother came to England with a women's group, and later that same summer their father was able to visit.

Anna returned to Vienna in 1950 to live with her parents and to study. In 1957, shortly after the death of her mother, she took vows and became a nun. After first studying economics at London University, Franz also decided to enter the church. He became a priest in the diocese of Westminster.

Courthouse, Vienna, Austria

Courtesy of the United States Holocaust Memorial Museum

---

3. The annexation of Austria into Nazi Germany.

EVA MOORE (NÉE WEITZMAN)

Eva was born in Vienna. Her father was a businessman. She had a brother, Walter. On December 31, 1936, her father died from a kidney disease. Now a widow, her mother took care of the family on her own. On March 12, 1938, Germany annexed Austria and immediately instituted anti-Semitic decrees. The following day, her mother sent Eva and Walter away to safety on a Kindertransport to France.

Courtesy of the United States Holocaust Memorial Museum

JEWISH REFUGEE CHILDREN

A small group of Jewish refugee children sitting outside in the grounds of the Priory, a children's home in Selkirk, Scotland.

Photo courtesy of the United States Holocaust Memorial Museum

Train Six

Kinder group gathered together for a photo. Top row: Dora, Bertha, unknown and Zelma. Seated: Rita, Frieda Korobkin and Ruth.

Courtesy of Freda Korobkin, Los Angeles, California, USA

ESTHER STAROBIN (NÉE ROSENFELD)

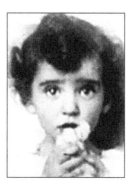

Esther was born in Adelsheim, Germany, on April 3, 1937. Her parents Katie and Adolf Rosenfeld had four other children: Bertl, Edith, Ruth and Herman. Esther's father sold feed and other products for cattle. Her mother helped him, as he had lost a leg in World War I. After they were no longer allowed to attend the local school, Esther's three older sisters went to live with relatives. In March 1939 her three sisters went to England on a Kindertransport. Esther herself was sent to England on a Kindertransport in June 1939. She was two years old.

Esther lived with Dorothy and Harry Harrison and their son Alan in Thorpe, Norwich, from 1939 until November 1947. She was very much part of this family. She went to school and the Harrisons gave her a happy childhood. Her sisters lived in a different part of England, but visited her whenever possible. Esther's parents and her brother were deported in October 1940 to the Gurs camp in France. Her brother was rescued in 1941 and came to the United States to live with an aunt and uncle. Esther's parents were sent to Auschwitz and murdered in August 1942.

Photo taken in the fall of 1938.
From left to right, Esther's brother Herman, her mother Kathi Lemberger Rosenfeld, Esther (on lap), Bertl, Edith, her father Adolf Rosenfeld and Ruth.

Esther Starobin
as an adult

In 1947 Esther, Bertl and Ruth went to the United States. Edith, at that time, was still in the British Army. When they first arrived in the US, they lived with an aunt and uncle. Edith eventually joined them. Edith and Bertl moved to an apartment with Esther. Both girls took great care of their younger sister Esther throughout her junior and senior high school years. Later, Esther lived with Ruth and her husband while in college at the University of Illinois where she studied to become a teacher.

United States Holocaust Memorial Museum,
courtesy of Esther Starobin

Train 7

HANS LEVY

OSKAR LEVY

Hans was born in February 1927 in Gladbeck, Germany. His brother Oskar was born in 1928 and his sister Elsbeth was born in 1925. Their parents owned a grocery store. During the Nazi boycott of Jewish businesses in 1933, the family store was vandalized. Soon afterward, the Levys sold the business and moved to Hamm. Hans and his siblings attended the local school, where they were tormented for being Jews.

Five years later, the family moved to Herzebrock, where they lived with relatives. During Kristallnacht on November 9-10, 1938, their house was ransacked and the boys' uncle was beaten. Immediately afterward, the boys' father and uncle fled to the home of another relative in Dortmund, returning only in mid-December. Hans and Oskar were registered on a Kindertransport bound for Holland. Elsbeth, who was thirteen years old at the time, left on a Kindertransport in January 1939. Hans and Oskar left one week later. The boys were moved several times before arriving in Amsterdam. Elsbeth moved in with German refugee relatives living in Amsterdam.

On February 17, 1940, all three siblings were together for Hans' Bar Mitzvah celebration. Three months later, Hans and Oskar sailed for England on the *SS Bodgraven* with sixty other Jewish refugee children. A few days after their arrival in Liverpool, they were taken to Manchester, where for the next eight years they resided in a hostel while attending school and working. In 1942 their parents were deported to Theresienstadt. Elsbeth, who was stranded in Amsterdam after the German invasion, was arrested in 1942 and sent to Theresienstadt, where she was reunited with her parents. She was later transferred to an ammunitions factory labor camp. From there, Elsbeth was deported to Auschwitz, where she learned her parents had arrived in October 1943 and had been killed immediately.

Elsbeth survived the war. Soon after the war she returned to Holland to marry her fiancé, Fred Kaufman, whom she had met in Theresienstadt. After just a brief search, she found Hans and Oskar in England. Elsbeth and her husband then immigrated to the United States. Hans and Oskar remained in England.

United States Holocaust Memorial Museum, courtesy of Hans Levy

LOTTE NUSSBAUM

Lotte, a young German Jewish girl, stayed in a children's home in Zuen, Belgium, after arriving on a Kindertransport.

United States Holocaust Memorial Museum, courtesy of Walter Reed

CHARLES SUSSKIND

Charles was born in Prague in August 1921. He left on a Kindertransport to England in August 1939. He was seventeen years old.

On the strength of an American visa, he parlayed his way into the US Armed Services and in 1945 immigrated to the United States with his British bride, Terry. As a beneficiary of the GI Bill, Charles completed his education and became a professor at UC Berkeley. Charles and Terry had three children. The youngest, Amanda, is the regional director of the Anti-Defamation League, the organization best known for fighting anti-Semitism and bigotry worldwide.

Prague, Czech Republic

Photo and text courtesy of Amanda Susskind,
regional director of the Anti-Defamation League, Los Angeles, California, USA

RITA HENNY GRATTER (NÉE SCHEINER)

Rita was born in Leipzig, Germany, in December 1925. She left on a Kindertransport to England and arrived at Liverpool Street Station in London in early May 1939.

Courtesy of Rita Henny Gratter, London, UK

BIANCA BRAVMANN

Bianca was born in Wittelshofen in Bayern, Germany, and at a young age moved to Munich to attend school there, after the children in Wittelshofen threw stones at her because she was Jewish. In 1939 Bianca and her cousin, Ruth Danzig, escaped on a Kindertransport to England.

United States Holocaust Memorial Museum, courtesy of Steven Franks

ELLEN ROTHSCHILD

ELLEN SCHAECHTER

Ellen Rothschild
Ellen Shaechter

German refugee children on the deck of the *SS Orama* en route to Australia in 1939. Amongst them are Ellen Rothschild and Ellen Schaechter.

United States Holocaust Memorial Museum, courtesy of Dr. Glen Palmer

PAUL KESTER

Although on a much smaller scale, some other European countries followed Britain's example and issued visas and provided refuge for small numbers of children. Sweden took in 500 children.

Paul was born in Wiesbaden, Germany, in December 1925. One of his relatives, a teacher at a Jewish refugee boarding school in Sweden that took in 40 of the 500 children, managed to arrange for Paul to be included. Paul traveled to Berlin on January 9, 1939, and obtained his visa at the Swedish consulate. On January 15, 1939, he went by train alone to southern Sweden to the boarding school. He stayed there until the age of 16. He then lived on his own in Stockholm for a number of years, escaping the fate of his parents and many of his family members and friends. He immigrated to the United States in early 1949.

He lives in Los Angeles with his wife Susanne. They have a son and two grandchildren.

Courtesy of Paul Kester, Los Angeles, California, USA

JOSEPHINE KNIGHT (NÉE EBERSTARK)

ALICE MASTERS (NÉE EBERSTARK)

ELLA APPLETON (NÉE EBERSTARK)

Josephine Knight   Alice Masters   Ella Appleton

Sidonia and Salamon Eberstark sent their three children, Josephine, Alice and Ella, to England on a Winton Kindertransport from Czechoslovakia on June 29, 1939. Josephine was fifteen, Alice was fourteen and Ella was ten.

This was written by Alice's daughter Kim when she was a teenager:

I never knew my mother's parents.
How they lived,
How they died
and why.

I can only imagine them
standing before me
frozen in the image
of a dusty brown photograph.

Left to right: Ella, Alice and Josephine

Vast, unswerving scourge,
Creators of hell on earth.
I curse you with all my being
For this robbery.

–Kim Masters, 1971

Seder Evening 1940

Written by Sidonia Eberstark to her children
from Trstena, Czechoslovakia, Passover 1940

Seder evening was lovely,
   once upon a time
when everyone was seated
   around the table.
Father always at the head
   and on either side
I, your mother and you
   my children,
eyes shining with happiness.
   Life was beautiful.
True joy indeed,
   because we were all together,
healthy and untroubled souls
sitting at the table, excitedly
   awaiting the festive night.
Father dips the bitter herbs
   and lets us taste them:

'Don't frown children,
   it is but a trifle compared
to the suffering
   of our forefathers.'
And so it goes on,
   all according to custom.
Father begins to tell
   the ancient story
'He lachma anya…'
   We all listen…
at the end the youngest
   at our Seder asks:
'Why is this night different
   from any other night?'
That's how it was before and
   that's how it was last year,
But this year you are not here,

Fate has forced us
  to send you to a foreign land.
Thank God your letters
  bring us good tidings,
but your empty seats embrace
  us with their emptiness.
Another Seder came,
  we sit down around the table.
There are only a few of us:
Father, mother and also
  your old granny,
whom fate forced from her
  home, her familiar place,
her children scattered
  helter-skelter.
Cruel fate touch us all.
And so we sit down once again
  to celebrate Seder
evening, mourning and tears in
  our eyes and a terrible ache
  in our hearts.
A great distance separates us…
  we think of you,
and you, dear children, think of
  us at the same moment.
We know that we are linked
  in thought and prayer.

In our hearts the firm belief
  that the time will come
when we will see each other
  again.
It will be like before –
  but a little different:
For you will have grown up,
  and we,
awaiting this precious moment,
  will have aged.
It will be beautiful
  as it once was:
We shall sit around
  the Seder table again
to celebrate our historic escape.
Don't despair children, fathers
  and mothers and all others:
The time will come
  when our suffering will end.
Dear brothers and sisters,
  do not despair, keep your faith,
  you will see your scattered
  families again.
God will protect and save us,
  the clouds will disperse,
And Eretz Israel will once again
  become our homeland.

Sidonia Eberstark, her husband Salomon, her sister Margit, and Salomon's 82-year-old mother were deported from their Slovak village on June 6, 1942.

Courtesy of Alice Masters, Bethseda, Maryland, USA

ANITA WEISBORD

Anita was born in Vienna and was the youngest of three. She had a wonderful childhood, loving parents, a big family and plenty of friends.

Life changed dramatically when Hitler marched into Austria in March 1938 and was welcomed with open arms, loud cheers of support and a frenzy of excitement by the Austrians. They were marching through the streets chanting, '*Hitler erwecke Jude verecke,*' which means 'Hitler awake, Jews perish'. At school, the girl who shared Anita's desk no longer talked to her. The neighbors she had known all her life no longer spoke to her. Hitler had already been in power in Germany for a few years. Every year another law was established against the Jews. Jews couldn't go to schools or universities, to the movies, or even sit on a park bench. In Austria in 1938 every law was put in place within twenty-four hours.

Then came Kristallnacht. Jewish stores were looted and synagogues were burned to the ground. Anita's father was arrested in their apartment and taken to the Dachau concentration camp. Furniture was smashed and their most cherished belongings were taken. Anita's mother realized that something had to be done quickly to save her children. Anita truly believes that her mother gave birth to her twice:

Anschluss – Hitler marches into Austria, March 1938.

Kristallnacht

when she was born, and when she gathered the strength to send her to safety on a Kindertransport.

Anita left Vienna in March 1939, one year after Hitler marched into Austria. She sat on the train for five agonizing hours as it stood there, with her mother outside watching and waiting. The train finally left and when it stopped at the German-Dutch border, heavily booted German border guards marched into her compartment and threatened that if any 'Jew kids' were smuggling jewelry or money, they would immediately be sent back. When they finally crossed over the border into Holland, they were greeted by wonderful Dutch women with sandwiches, lemonade and chocolate. Anita married in London and came to the United States in 1947. She has two children, four granddaughters and a happy and productive life.

Courtesy of Anita Weisbord, Douglaston, New York, USA

TRAUTE MORGENSTERN

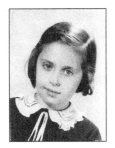

Traute was born in January 1929. She left Vienna on a Kindertransport with her brother Peter in early December 1938. She and her brother stayed with wonderful guardians, but after the outbreak of war, she was evacuated to various foster parents from all over the countryside. In 1947 she was reunited with her parents who had managed to survive in Italy. Traute has been living in Italy ever since, and has remained very close to her brother and all his family in England.

Courtesy of Traute Morgenstern, Milan, Italy

PETER MORGAN (FORMERLY MORGENSTERN)

Peter was born in October 1930. He was eight years old when he left with his sister Traute on one of the first Kindertransports out of Vienna in early December 1938. He had wonderful guardians, but after the outbreak of war, he was evacuated to various foster parents all over the countryside. When he was naturalized in 1951, he changed his surname to Morgan, the name that his guardians had adopted for him soon after his arrival.

Courtesy of Traute Morgenstern, Milan, Italy

HEINZ STEPHAN LEWY

Heinz was born in Berlin in March 1925. He was just fourteen years old in July 1939, when he left Berlin on a Kindertransport to France, where a group of children were given refuge in a castle in the town of Quincy near Paris. In early 1942 Heinz was able, with the help of his parents, to secure a visa and he made his way to Casablanca, Morocco, where he then sailed to New York with a large group of Jewish refugee children.

United States Holocaust Memorial Museum, courtesy of Stephan H. Lewy

THREE *KINDER*

Three Jewish Girl Scouts in England who were living in the Selkirk Priory.
All came to Scotland on the Kindertransport. Date unknown.

United States Holocaust Memorial Museum, courtesy of Susanne Spritzer Perl

HANS KLEIN

Hans was born in Prague in April 1924. He left Czechoslovakia on a Winton train in 1939. Hans joined a *Hachshara* – a kibbutz-style agricultural preparation training program – in Swimbridge in Devon, England.

Courtesy of the United States Holocaust Memorial Museum

LORE JACOBS (NÉE GOTTHELF)

Lore was born in April 1924 in Frankfurt. After Kristallnacht, her family applied to immigrate to the United States but since their application numbers were high and the wait was very long, Lore was registered for a Kindertransport to England. She was accepted and left Germany in July 1939. Her sponsors were the Quakers of Northampton, England. Lore's parents were deported to Lodz in October 1941, where they perished.

Frankfurt, Germany

United States Holocaust Memorial Museum, courtesy of Lore Gotthelf

Train Nine

55

VERA RATTNER (NÉE SINGER)

Vera was born in Berlin in July 1924. She left Berlin on one of the last Kindertransports in August 1939, just weeks before the war broke out. Upon her arrival in England, she and a group of young Jewish refugees disembarked from the ship and were taken to a transit camp in Kent. After about two weeks, they were sent to their final destination: a small town in north Wales called Abergele. They stayed in Gwrych Castle, by the sea. The castle's surroundings were beautiful but there was no electricity and it was freezing cold in the winter.

Vera was part of a group called the *Bachad* Movement (Movement of Religious Pioneers)[4]. She stayed there for over two years. Some of the youngsters went to hostels and some to farms to be trained in agriculture. Throughout Britain, there were many organized centers that took in groups of youngsters. Vera was sent to a farm where she was treated very well. She stayed there a short time because her parents had managed to get to London where they had settled, and soon she was able to join them. Vera stayed in England until 1948, when she decided to go to Israel, where she settled very happily. Her parents joined her toward the end of 1950.

Vera married and has two children, four grandchildren and five great-grandchildren.

Courtesy of Vera Rattner, Kfar Saba, Israel

BERTA (SCHECK) WESLER

Berta was born in Dortmund, Germany, in 1928. She was one of seven children. In December 1938, ten-year-old Berta and her sister Klara, aged twelve, left Dortmund on a Kindertransport via Holland, and then by ship to England. Her younger sister joined them nine months later. Her older brother was brought over by her guardians.

Dortmund, Germany

Courtesy of Berta (Scheck) Wesler, Walnut Creek, California, USA

---

4. The *Bachad* Movement raised money in the UK and provided agriculture and education training for *Bnei Akiva*, a Zionist youth movement.

Dorothy (Dorli) was born in 1928 and Lisi was born in 1934, both in Vienna. In March 1938 the Nazis had taken over Austria and the cruel treatment of Vienna's Jews got progressively worse. All the lovely things that Dorli enjoyed doing with her sister Lisi were becoming impossible. Dorli was ten years old and Lisi was aged just four. Their father had both his optician shops taken away and Dorli had been forced to leave her high school. As a Jewish family, they were being treated in the harshest way and they continually heard about the awful things that were happening to other Jewish families, just like theirs.

Her parents got to hear about the Kindertransport and made the brave and heartbreaking decision to let Dorli and Lisi go. The girls left Vienna on a Kindertransport on January 10, 1939, arriving in London two days later. For Dorli, going to England felt like an adventure, and looking after and caring for her young sister had always been her ambition.

A lovely Jewish couple in Leeds, Theo and Tilly Hall, agreed to take them in and by doing so, surely saved their lives. They were allowed to take one piece of luggage each to England and nothing of great value in it. The most precious thing Dorli had with her was her autograph book. On the first page, her father had drawn a reminder of her life so far – all the things she did and hoped for – and she still to this day laughs and cries when she looks at it. She and her sister had an adventurous journey and arrived safely in England. They settled in well with Tilly and Theo. Dorli could speak English, but Lisi couldn't, so it was much harder for her as she was so young and missed her parents dreadfully. How fortunate Dorli and Lisi were that their parents did manage to get out later.

Dorothy's autograph book

Both girls were evacuated to different places because of the war, but in 1941 they finally came together as a family. Lisi had a sad life, but Dorli had a good career and married a fellow refugee from Vienna. Dorli had three children, six grandchildren and now, four great-grandchildren, and they all know her story and will tell it to their children. Dorli always articulates how we all need to know the dreadful things humans can do to each other, but we also need to know that brave and kind people exist too, and we need to learn from them.

Changes
by Dorothy Fleming

All of a sudden the atmosphere changed;
At home it grew quiet, the laughter all gone.
At school we were outcasts:
'Don't talk to them—they're Jewish!'
the teacher said; she who'd liked me before.

The friends who wrote in my autograph book
Were no longer friends, wore uniforms now;
Bund Deutscher Mädchen—Hitler Youth,
In my school, in my town, strangers to me.

All of a sudden the atmosphere changed;
No longer talk of music, of plays, and of fun.
Now it was permits and visas and death;

Friends going missing, lucky ones left,
Less lucky those who were taken away—
Who could know where and for what?

Streets full of danger, new banners and flags
Frightening because no one explained
What it all meant, what would come next.

All of a sudden the atmosphere changed;
'There're people in England who'll give you a home
Until we get out and join you again—
You'll get the chance to practice your English
And live with an uncle and auntie in Leeds
And take care of your little sister.'

Train journey of fears and surprises
We remember the smiling and kindly Dutch
And arriving in smoky London; for some it was all too much.
All of a sudden the atmosphere changed;
In Yorkshire now, long way from home.

Strange names and bedrooms and breakfasts;
Phone calls from Vienna to Chapeltown, Leeds:
'Are you sure you're looking after your sister?
Behaving yourselves and learning at school?

Is Lisi still crying, still wetting her bed?
We'll come to you soon, just wait a bit more
And thank Uncle Theo and give Tilly a kiss!'

All of a sudden the atmosphere changed.
Settled in Leeds now, the plaits an attraction;
Sister's calmed down, and school can be fun,
Dancing round maypole, learning some folk songs,
But arithmetic's agony, all those long sums!

Parents are coming! Longed-for reunion
Big hugs and kisses—and then they are gone! And
All of a sudden the atmosphere changed.

War comes and evacuation—travelling all over
This surprising new country of ours.
Where can we settle? Father's interned.
Now he's an enemy alien, who loves this country so much.

At last we're all together in Wales.
War work for Daddy and new schools for us;
No longer refugees, evacuees or any ees,
Just two girls growing up and seeing that
All of a sudden the atmosphere changed.

Many years later, we suddenly found out
That Kindertransport had been what saved us.
We'd been the lucky ones, our parents survived;
Most of the children were orphaned.

Terrible memories suddenly stirred
Some could hardly believe it;
Friendships renewed, experiences shared
With families now and emotions bared—and
All of a sudden the atmosphere changed.

Courtesy of Dorothy Fleming, Sheffield, South Yorkshire, UK

KINDER GROUP ON THE FIRST TRANSPORT

Courtesy of the United States Holocaust Memorial Museum

SHERRARDS BOYS HOSTEL

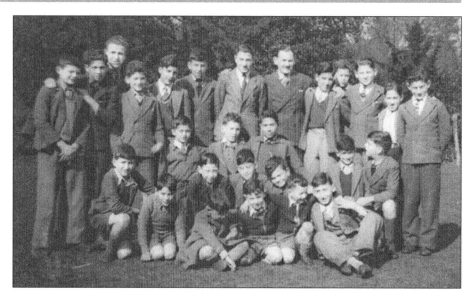

Courtesy of the United States Holocaust Memorial Museum

RUTH ADAMECZ

Ruth was born in Breslau, Germany, in April 1932. She had two sisters, Inge and Gretl. Their mother sent Ruth and Inge to England on a Kindertransport. Both girls arrived at Liverpool Street Station in early 1939. Ruth was seven years old and her sister Inge was just five years old. They stayed at a Jewish refugee hostel in Tynemouth near Newcastle and later were evacuated to Windermere in the Lake District. Their younger sister Gretl did not leave on a Kindertransport. Sadly, she and her mother perished.

In 1953 Ruth and Inge immigrated to Israel. They both married. Ruth was a member of a kibbutz (communal farm) in the south of the country. Inge eventually moved back to England. Ruth has two sons: one living in the USA and one in Israel.

Photo courtesy of United States Holocaust Memorial Museum
Text courtesy of Alisa Tennenbaum, Bet Cherut, Israel

GERHARD ALEXANDER

Gerhard was a German Jewish refugee who was sent to France on a Kindertransport in the spring of 1939.

United States Holocaust Memorial Museum,
courtesy of Stephan H. Lewy

FRANK MEISLER

Frank was born in Danzig, Germany, on December 29, 1925. He left Germany on a Kindertransport in August 1939 and traveled with fourteen other Jewish children via Berlin to the Netherlands and then to his final destination, Liverpool Street Station in London. In total, four Kindertransport journeys were made from his city; Frank was on the last and it saved his life. The day he left, German soldiers had already infiltrated what was then the Free City of Danzig. Days later, his parents were arrested and held in the Warsaw Ghetto and they were subsequently deported to Auschwitz. He attended school in London and graduated with a degree in architecture from Manchester University. In 1960 he settled in Israel and made his home and studio in the Artist's Quarter of the Old City of Jaffa.

In 2006 his sculpture group 'Children of the Kindertransport' was erected in Hope Square, Liverpool Street Station, unveiled by Prince Charles. Two additional sculpture groups commemorating the departure and journey of the Kindertransport: 'Trains to Life, Trains to Death' and 'Kindertransport – the Departure' were erected in Berlin and Gdansk in 2008 and 2009. In 2011 he unveiled a public sculpture in the port of Rotterdam, Holland 'Channel Crossing to Life'.

Courtesy of Frank Meisler, Jaffa, Israel

Gunther was born in Berlin in October 1926. His father, Wilhelm, was a lawyer who committed suicide soon after the Nazi takeover of Germany in 1933. Gunther's mother, Kathe Lubczinski Abrahamson, was from Posen (Poznan), Poland. She took care of Gunther and his older sister, Daisy, who was born in September 1921. Daisy immigrated to Palestine in 1938, and in July 1939 Gunther was sent on a Kindertransport to England. Gunther corresponded with his mother via the Red Cross, but in 1942 she was deported to Riga, Latvia. She did not survive World War II.

On arrival in England, Gunther and several other children on the same Kindertransport went first to a transit camp in Barham House near Ipswich. From there they were dispersed across the United Kingdom. Gunther and two other boys were sent to Selkirk in Scotland. Before the arrival of the refugee children, the Priory served as a holiday home for children from under-privileged homes in Edinburgh, Scotland. The matron of the house, Margaret Mackie, imposed strict discipline on all the children, regardless of age. Gunther, who was thirteen years old at the time, disliked the atmosphere at the Priory. A local minister arranged for him to work at a nearby farm that belonged to the Millar Family. He stayed with them until 1946, when he left to study at the University of Edinburgh. After graduation, he left Britain and in 1952 he settled in Canada and currently resides in Ottawa.

Gunther and his lead dog on the Tundra near Tuktoyaktuk, Northwest Territories, Canada (1960).

Photo and text courtesy of Gunther Abrahamson, Ottawa, Ontario, Canada

Train Eleven

EDITH ROSENTHAL (NÉE GOLDAPPER)

Edith was a young Jewish refugee in a children's home in Zuen, Brussels. Some children went to this home on a Kindertransport.

United States Holocaust Memorial Museum, courtesy of Walter Reed

ANITA HOFFER (NÉE LÖWENBERG)

Anita was born in Berlin in June 1933. Her parents divorced when she was three years old and she and her mother went to live with her maternal grandparents. She was six when she left on a Kindertransport to England on June 23, 1939. Fortunately, her mother was able to join her quite soon after she arrived and she took Anita out of the unhappy environment in which she had been living. Her mother found a job as a housekeeper, intending that Anita would be able to live with her. That lasted just one week.

Anita's passport

With no choice, Anita went to live in an orphanage. She did not see her mother again until about two years later, when her mother went to the home of a wonderful woman, Ms. A.D. Scott, who had taken Anita in after she had lived for about three months in the orphanage. Ms. Scott's home was filled with

Anita in her school uniform

Anita's ID document

other children, mainly British, whose parents were unable to take care of them during the difficult wartime years in Britain. Anita received occasional letters from her mother, but she was considered an enemy alien[5] so could not travel to see Anita or call on the phone – even her letters were censored.

Anita lived there happily for about two years until her mother came, just prior to Pearl Harbor, and said she had visas for the United States where her parents had settled. Anita was devastated to leave Ms. Scott.

Anita settled in New Jersey and lived with her maternal grandparents through high school. She had a successful career, married and had two wonderful children and grandchildren.

Forty-two years after Anita left Germany, she was reunited with her father. He had remarried and spent the war years in Shanghai. After the war he had returned to Germany and worked as an attorney, but later he moved to Los Angeles, where he settled.

Anita is the president of the Florida Chapter of the KTA (Kindertransport Association).

Courtesy of Anita Hoffer,
Boca Raton, Florida, USA

5. An enemy alien is a citizen of a country that is in a state of conflict with the land in which he or she is located. Usually, but not always, the countries are in a state of declared war.

Train 12

THEO MARKUS VERDERBER

Theo was born in Cologne, Germany, in June 1928. In February 1939 Theo was lucky enough to be selected to join a Kindertransport and on February 15, 1939, he arrived in England. He later immigrated to Israel. His mother, sister and youngest brother remained in Europe and perished near Krakow in 1942. His older brother, Israel Moses, survived and immigrated to Israel.

Courtesy of the United States Holocaust Memorial Museum

ASAF AUERBACH

Asaf was born on May 28, 1928, in Ein Harod, Palestine (now Israel). But in 1930 his parents returned with him and his brother to Czechoslovakia, which is how they eventually became 'Nicholas Winton's children'. They left on the second-to-last transport on July 18, 1939, and arrived in London on July 20.

Courtesy of Asaf Auerbach, Prague, Czech Republic

MIMI ALICE ORMOND (NÉE SCHLEISSNER)

Mimi was born in January 1926 in Marienbad, in the Sudetenland region of Czechoslovakia. In May 1939, when she was thirteen years old, she left on a Winton Kindertransport to England. Her older brother, Edi, was not able to join her as he was too old at age eighteen. Mimi only planned to stay in England for a few months, but Germany's invasion of Poland on September 1, 1939, and the start of World War II caused her to remain in Britain until the end of the war. In December 1939 Mimi's parents and brother managed to leave Czechoslovakia and reached Palestine in January 1940. In 1942 Mimi left the agriculture training program she was attending and moved in with her aunt and uncle in Cheltenham, where she was tutored in English by a refugee professor. He told her that if she wanted to train to become a nursery teacher, she could attend college for free. After two years of study, she became a head nurse in a day-care center and entered a lifelong career in early childhood education. Mimi met American soldier and violinist Edward Ormond and they married in November 1944. Before settling in the United States, Mimi traveled to Palestine to visit her parents and her brother. After the reunion with her immediate family, she traveled to Egypt and then sailed to the United States on board the *SS Thomas Barry*.

United States Holocaust Memorial Museum, courtesy of Mimi Alice Schleissner

PETER KOLLISCH

EVA KOLLISCH

Peter, Eva and Stephen (see page 172) Kollisch were sent by their parents on a Kindertransport from Vienna in July 1939. They all stayed

with a Quaker family in Bristol for six months before receiving immigration papers to the United States. When they arrived in the USA in March 1940, the Kollisch siblings were reunited with their parents, who had fled Vienna in the fall of 1939.

Eva and Peter Kollisch

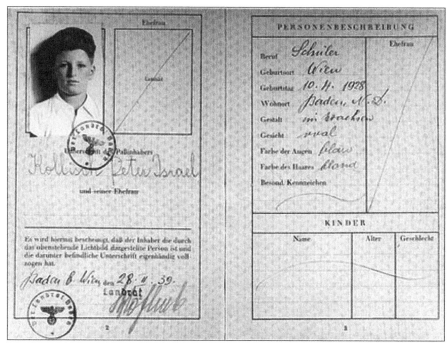

Peter Kollisch passport courtesy of the United States Holocaust Memorial Museum.

United States Holocaust Memorial Museum, courtesy of Peter Kollisch

SIR NICHOLAS WINTON

(Kindertransport Rescuer)

In December 1938 Nicholas Winton was living in London and working as a stockbroker. He was twenty-nine years old. He had made plans to go on a two-week skiing vacation with his friend, Martin Blake, a teacher at Westminster School. Before the scheduled trip, Blake was in Prague visiting his friend Doreen Warriner, who was the city's first representative of the British Committee for Refugees from Czechoslovakia. He was introduced to the mounting crisis of the dire conditions in which refugee families were being forced to live, and he called Winton and asked him to cancel their planned skiing vacation and join him in Prague. Winton readily agreed.

In Prague Winton met the most important people involved with the refugee rescue. He went to refugee camps and saw for himself the terrible conditions in which these children were living, and decided to establish his own rescue operation. He set up an office at the hotel in Wenceslas Square, where he was staying, and started interviewing parents. Before long, parents were lining up to meet him, begging him to include their children on his lists and take them to safety in England.

When Winton arrived back in London, he came with a suitcase full of photos of children and lists of their names. He went back to work and, at the end of each day, he devoted his time to his rescue mission. He formed an organization that consisted of himself, his mother, his secretary and a few volunteers. He placed advertisements in newspapers and wrote requests wherever he could all over the country, looking for British families willing to take in these children. He persuaded the Home Office to let the children into the country and worked very closely with the officials issuing entry permits.

Before he left Prague, his first transport was a planeload of children to Croydon, England. This was funded by the Barbican Mission and Winton took care of the logistics. He posed as a journalist so that he could carry a young boy, Hansi Neumann, onto the aircraft. Hansi was three years old. The plane landed at Croydon Airport and from there the children were taken by bus to the Barbican Mission's residential home in Brockley. Tragically, little Hansi died in the Mission home of an inner ear infection and his parents disappeared in the concentration camps.

Nicholas Winton with Hansi Neumann at Ruzyne Airport on January 12, 1939, just before the KLM flight took off for Reading, England. Little Hansi was just three years old.

The first transport left from Prague in March 1939, and Winton subsequently organized seven more transports out of Prague's Wilson Railway Station (now Prague Main Station), which all arrived safely in England. Some children got off the train at Harwich and were met by local people; most of the children were met at London's Liverpool Street Station by their new families. What was to be his last transport with the most children – about 250 – was due to leave the day the war broke out. That transport went in the opposite direction. The fate of those children is unknown.

Nicholas Winton brought 669 children to safety. These children became known as the 'Winton Children'. One of the most remarkable aspects of his rescue efforts is that his bravery and good deeds were unknown by all, except by those directly involved until fifty years later, when his wife Greta found a briefcase in the attic of their home in London. It contained a scrapbook with details and photos of each child that he saved. She notified the newspapers and TV stations. In 1988 they were both invited to appear on a BBC television program called *That's Life*. The program's famous presenter,

Esther Rantzen, had managed, without Winton's knowledge, to track down about 200 of the 669 children he had saved. Although Nicholas Winton had saved their lives, these children, now adults with their own families, had no idea who he was.

Today, there are well over five thousand people who are part of his rescued children's families, living all over the world.

In 1983 Winton was awarded an MBE[6]. In 2002 he was knighted by Queen Elizabeth II and became Sir Nicholas Winton.

Sir Nicholas Winton celebrated his 105th birthday on May 19, 2014. He is the oldest living rescuer of the Holocaust and a true British humanitarian.

Nicholas Winton saved 669 children. The number of decendants continues to grow, and today amounts to over 5,000. These are the thirty-seven 'Winton Children' whose stories appear in this book.

6. MBE: Member of the Order of the British Empire, a British honor given to a person by the monarch for a particular achievement.

Train 13

ELIAS JAFFE

Elias Jaffe left on a Kindertransport to England in July 1939 from Danzig, Germany.

Danzig, Germany

Courtesy of Michelle Jaffe, London, UK

Several Jewish organizations assisted the refugee children. When they arrived in Britain, the children were housed in temporary reception camps, such as

Two young refugee boys having a meal at the Pakefield Holiday Camp in Suffolk, England.

Dovercourt Bay, Pakefield and Broadstairs holiday camps. After a few weeks, they were taken to foster homes or hostels throughout the country. Others lived on agricultural training farms set up by the Youth Aliyah organization in Britain.

Courtesy of the Institute of National Remembrance, Poland

ERIC SEIF

Eric Seif was just fourteen years old in 1939 when he left Vienna on a Kindertransport to England.

Courtesy of Eric Seif, Granada Hills, California, USA

TWO AUSTRIAN REFUGEE CHILDREN

Two Austrian refugee children on a Kindertransport on their arrival at Harwich, England.

Courtesy of Bibliotheque Historique de la Ville de Paris, France

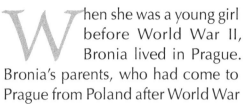

When she was a young girl before World War II, Bronia lived in Prague. Bronia's parents, who had come to Prague from Poland after World War I, started a small film distributing business. Films were the new industry, rather like the computer industry today. Worrying news began reaching Prague from Germany of the hatred toward the Jews. In March 1938 Hitler took control of Austria and immediately started implementing his anti-Jewish laws. Old men were made to scrub the pavements with toothbrushes, while onlookers watched and jeered. In September of that year, the Munich Agreement was signed by Germany, France, the United Kingdom and Italy, whereby Hitler was given all the northern territories (called the Sudetenland) that he had been demanding, because the majority of the inhabitants were German speaking. Suddenly, there were enemies at the borders.

Old Jewish men were made to scrub the pavement with toothbrushes.

Even as an eleven-year-old, Bronia was aware of what was going on. Her parents were frantically discussing how and where to escape. All too soon, the atmosphere changed and life became one of fear. One day, Bronia found herself packing. It had been arranged that she would go to some cousins of her mother's who lived in London and stay there and wait for her parents to come and meet her, and as a family they would go to the United States. She was allowed to take just a few of her most precious possessions. She chose her doll, a favorite book, her piano music and her autograph album, which had wonderful poems and messages written in it by friends and family. Her mother added a few special belongings so she wouldn't arrive empty-handed to her new family.

When Bronia arrived at the railway station in Prague, it was full with parents and children and German soldiers. Bronia remembers being very scared. She and the other children got on the train, it started moving and parents and children frantically waved at each other. It never occurred to anyone that they would never see one another again. Once the train crossed the border into Holland, Bronia and the other children on the train knew they were safe.

Bronia with her parents

Bronia with her brother Leo

Bronia arrived in England at the beginning of June 1939. Her parents wrote frequently, describing the increasingly restrictive measures being imposed on them as Jews. They had to wear the Yellow Star when out in the street; they were not permitted to enter parks, sit on benches, go to swimming pools, restaurants, cinemas or hospitals; they were not permitted to own radios, and so much more.

One morning, as Bronia was getting ready for school, she received a letter informing her that her parents and brother had been transported from Theresienstadt to Auschwitz and that they had not survived. This was a devastating blow. It was the end of all her hopes and dreams that had been centered on her being reunited one day with her family. She was suddenly faced with the realization that she was alone. Bronia decided that she would do her best to live up to her parents' example and expectations and be 'happy' because they had made such a brave decision to send her away to a strange country and to strangers so that she would be happy. Bronia continued her studies and worked, and she married and had two sons.

On Friday, September 4, 2009, twenty-two *kinder* were reunited with their 'savior', Sir Nicholas Winton, who was then one hundred years old.

Courtesy of Bronia Snow, Esher, Surrey, UK

I ngrid, her sister Annelore and brother Hans arrived to England from Hamburg, Germany on a Kindertransport in 1939.

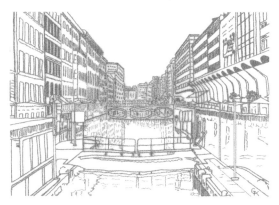

Hamburg, Germany

Ingrid with her rucksack

Ingrid with her sister Annalore and brother Hans

Courtesy of Vally Kovary, Ithaca, New York, USA

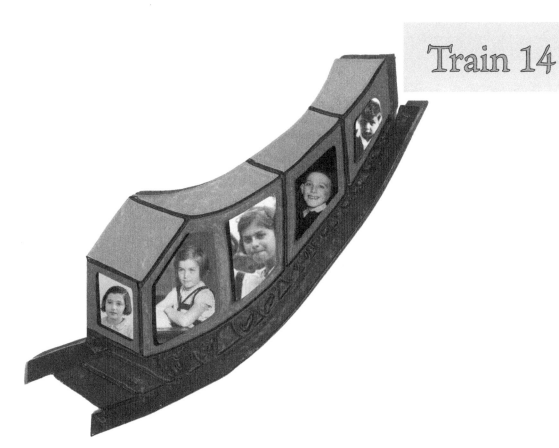

IRENE WATTS (NÉE KIRSTEIN)

Irene was born in Berlin in 1931. She was just seven years old when she was taken to safety on a Kindertransport, arriving in England on December 10, 1938. In August 1968 Irene immigrated to Canada, where she became a teacher. She worked in Theater for Young Audiences, writing and directing plays for professional actors to perform in schools all over Canada.

Irene is a writer/playwright who has worked throughout Canada and Europe. She has been awarded numerous honors. Her three historical novels for young people about the Kindertransport, *Goodbye Marianne*, *Remember Me*, and *Finding Sophie*, were republished in an omnibus edition to mark the 75th Anniversary of Kindertransport, under the title *Escape from Berlin*.

Courtesy of Irene Watts, Vancouver, British Columbia, Canada

ERICH GOLDSTEIN

E rich left on a Kindertransport out of Berlin through Holland on December 1, 1938. He became a famous violinist.

RALPH SAMUEL

R alph was born in Dresden, Germany, in 1931. He was only seven and a half years old when he was sent alone on a Kindertransport to England and forced to say goodbye to his family. Unusually, Ralph traveled to England by airplane.

Ralph Samuel was met at Croydon Airport in London by Samuel Epstein, who had selected him from a list because they both had the name 'Samuel'. In addition, Samuel Epstein had a son called Peter, whose middle name was Ralph. So it was simply due to these coincidences that Ralph went to the Epstein family.

Ralph's mother, Ellen, wrote to Mr. Epstein about how bad things had become in Germany. In March 1939 Ellen was hired as a live-in maid by the Epstein family. Ralph clearly remembers that he ate dinner in the dining room with the family while his mother ate in the kitchen.

In November 1939 Ralph's father was sent to the Buchenwald concentration camp. He was released after six weeks. Three years later he was sent to Hellerberg, a work camp near Dresden, and in March 1943 he was deported to Auschwitz, where he perished. Ralph's grandmother was sent to the Theresienstadt concentration camp in August 1942 and died that year.

When he was twenty-seven, Ralph immigrated to the United States. In 1962 he moved to California. His mother joined him and spent the last 15 years of her life in Oakland.

Today, Ralph is involved with various Kindertransport groups. He helped found the northern California chapter of the Kindertransport

Association and has attended many of their reunions. He also volunteers in the Speakers Bureau for the Holocaust Center of Northern California and has spoken at many schools in California and in Germany.

Ralph with Denise (Peter's sister), Mrs. Epstein and Peter, summer 1939.

Ralph with Samuel Epstein and Peter, Bournemouth, UK, 1941.

Courtesy of Ralph Samuel, Oakland, California, USA

SYLVIA ABRAMOVICI

Sylvia was a German Jewish refugee child who had arrived in England on a Kindertransport and stayed at the *B'nai B'rith*[7] hostel in Hackney, London.

United States Holocaust Memorial Museum, courtesy of Ruth Wasserman Segal

7. *B'nai B'rith* is the oldest Jewish service organization in the world and is the global voice of the Jewish community. It is the most widely known Jewish humanitarian and human rights advocacy organization. It is committed to the security and continuity of the Jewish people and the State of Israel and combating anti-Semitism and bigotry. Its mission is to unite persons of the Jewish faith and to enhance Jewish identity.

Maggy was born in Berlin in 1928. She arrived in England on a Kindertransport in January 1939. She lived with a Jewish family and attended boarding school for a few years. In 1953 Maggy met her American husband during a trip to Paris. They lived in New York for about seven years before moving to California, where they have lived for over fifty years, enjoying their two daughters and four grandchildren.

Berlin, Germany

Courtesy of Maggy Prost, California, USA

LISA HILL (NÉE E. FUERTH)

Lisa was just ten years old when she traveled to England from Prague in June 1939 on one of Sir Nicholas Winton's trains. In January 1946 she returned to Prague on a similar long train journey, this time across devastated Germany in the company of English war brides of Czech soldiers. Lisa had one thing in common with them: she, too, could not speak Czech. In the years that she was away, she had forgotten her mother tongue. Lisa's parents, who greeted her at the station, seemed like strangers. In so many ways, returning was as difficult as the long separation had been. Three years later, following the communist coup, she had to leave once again, when as a family they immigrated to Canada, settling first in Hamilton and later in Toronto. In the years since, Lisa married and had two daughters and two grandsons.

Courtesy of Lisa Hill

John Rosen (formerly Hans Rosenbaum) and his older brother Walter were born near Buer, Germany. They were put on a Kindertransport by their parents on March 15, 1939, when John was eight and Walter was ten. They arrived with all the other children on the train at Liverpool Street Station from where they were collected by Mr Farrell, a colleague of Mr Alan Sainsbury (who later became Lord Sainsbury) and his wife Babette.

Their selection must have been quite random as none of the children had any connections in England. John and Walter were accommodated in a large detached house in Putney, west London. There they were looked after by a domestic staff, including a matron, and English and Hebrew teachers. They shared a room with two other brothers. John remembers that although most of the children were on their own, there was another group of two girls and two boys from the same family.

They were looked after in the most generous way by Mr. Sainsbury and his friends, who obviously funded everything. They were often visited by 'Mr. Alan', as he came to be called, and Mrs. Sainsbury, and other friends of theirs. They were taken in small groups to visit the zoo and other places of interest in London. In the summer the whole group was taken to the seaside for a holiday.

All the children were provided with clothing, medical care and even individual pocket money of 'tuppence' per week. They were able to correspond with their parents in Germany and received their mail as well. Obviously they hoped their parents would be able to leave Germany. John remembers how he and Walter tried to save some of their pocket money to give them when they arrived. They were particularly fortunate that their parents did manage to escape to London just one week before the outbreak of war.

They must have learned to speak English very quickly and soon they were all escorted to the local school. Shortly after the outbreak of war, the entire school including John and Walter, the 'Sainsbury children', were evacuated to Reading in the special care of the headmaster – Mr. Cook and his wife. They were all billeted in various private homes in keeping with what happened to all the evacuees.

At this point in their lives, the Sainsbury children were spread all over the Reading area and most of them lost contact with one another. Mr. Cook, on behalf of Mr. Sainsbury, continued to monitor their individual progress and as before they were all provided with clothing when necessary. Their weekly pocket money increased to sixpence, and this continued until they reached school leaving age. With the exception of John and Walter, it is thought that all the 'Sainsbury children' lost their parents during the Holocaust.

John and Walter were fortunate to see their parents very occasionally when they visited them for a few hours – they themselves were struggling to make a living in their very reduced circumstances, having arrived in England with just one case and ten shillings! John and Walter remained evacuated until the end of the war, by which time their parents had progressed from living in a furnished room to a rented apartment and they were finally reunited as a family again.

During the entire war period and beyond, Mr. Sainsbury, on behalf of the 'Sainsbury Committee', maintained a close interest in the welfare of the children and received regular reports relating to their education and the early years of their employment. Mr. Sainsbury sent them birthday cards each year with a special gift on their 21st birthday, and similarly sent a gift for Walter's wedding in 1958. John and Walter, together with Walter's wife Valerie, visited the then Lord Sainsbury on a number of occasions in his London office, where they were received with great kindness. John and Walter will always remember with gratitude the tremendous part Lord Sainsbury and his committee played in looking after all of the children during those very difficult days.

John immigrated to the United States in 1952 and after serving in the Army became an American citizen and made his life there. John has continued to remember his wartime experiences as a Kindertransport child. In 1942 Walter was sent to Guildford, where he attended a technical school. Walter lived in London with his wife, two children and grandchildren.

Courtesy of John Rosen, Michigan/Florida, USA

PETER WEGNER (FORMERLY WEIDEN-WEGNER)

Peter was born on August 20, 1932. On April 25, 1939, his grandmother put him on a Kindertransport train in Vienna. His mother had fled to England a year earlier, as she was on a 'wanted list' issued by the Nazis immediately after the *Anschluss*.

Peter's train arrived at Liverpool Street Station in London on April 27, 1939.

Courtesy of Judith Romney Wegner, Providence, Rhode Island, USA

KINDER CHILDREN ARRIVING AT HARWICH

A group photo of the first 200 Kindertransport children arriving by ship
at the East Anglian Port of Harwich, England, in December 1938.
Most of the transports left by train from Vienna, Berlin, Prague and other major cities.
Children living in smaller towns traveled to meet the transports,
crossed the Dutch and Belgian borders and went on by ship to England.

Courtesy of United States Holocaust Memorial Museum

Richard was born in 1929. In March 1939 he left Leipzig, Germany, traveling by train to Holland and by boat to Harwich, England, and then boarding another train to London. He was nine years old. He went to live in the home of a truly remarkable family who took good care of him. One of their five children, John Schlesinger, would later become a famous film director, known for such pictures as *Midnight Cowboy* and *Marathon Man*. Richard's mother and sister fled to Holland and then in August 1939 to England, boarding the last KLM plane before the outbreak of war. He was one of the very fortunate few to be reunited with at least one parent.

In October 2009 Richard was invited to Leipzig. It was his first visit back since he left in 1939. A film was made about him and shown on German television. Richard has now written about this incredible journey, which was a transformative experience for him.

Leipzig, Germany

Text extracts courtesy of the Syracuse University Magazine.
H. Richard Levy is a professor emeritus of biology.
He retired in 2000 after thirty-seven years at the university.

Train Fifteen

TWO BRITISH QUAKER WOMEN

Two British Quaker women, who served as foster parents to Jewish
Kindertransport children, pose with a group of young children in Bristol, England.

United States Holocaust Memorial Museum, courtesy of Peter Kollisch

RUTH OFNEROVA

HANA OFNEROVA

Ruth was ten when she left on the Czech Kindertransport with her sister Hana, aged fourteen. Both sisters and their cousin, Eva, arrived in London July 1, 1939.

Courtesy of Susan Waite (daughter of Hana Ofnerova), Victoria, Australia

EVA BONN

Eva was the cousin of Ruth and Hana Ofnerova. She was born in December 1924. Eva was fifteen years old when she left Prague with her two cousins on the Czech Kindertransport, arriving in London July 1, 1939.

Courtesy of Susan Waite

SABINE LANDAU (NÉE STANG)

Sabine left Berlin on a Kindertransport on August 10, 1939 and arrived at Liverpool Street Station in London. She spent the next couple of years in various hostels, including Gwrych Castle, north Wales. In 1941 Sabine went on *Hachshara* near Buckinghamshire under the auspices of *Bachad,* an organization that raised money in the UK and provided agricultural and educational training for the Bnei Akiva Zionist youth movement. In 1944 she went to Rowledge near Aldershot to help look after Jewish evacuee children. After the war ended, Sabine went to Windermere in the Lake District to help look after children who survived the Holocaust. From there, she moved to a hostel in Great Chesterford to help look after girls who survived the Holocaust.

In 1946 Sabine moved to London as a trainee dressmaker. She married Manfred Landau, who was also originally from Berlin, on January 19, 1947.

Courtesy of Susan Lew (daughter of Sabine and Manfred Landau), London, UK

MANFRED LANDAU

Manfred left Berlin on the first Kindertransport on December 1, 1938, and arrived at Harwich, England, via the Hook of Holland. He spent about two weeks in a boys hostel at Dovercourt and then transferred to another camp at Lowestoft.

On January 1, 1939, he was moved to his first 'permanent house', which was a hostel in Leeds where he stayed with two of his brothers until about 1942. From Leeds, Manfred went on *Hachshara* to a hostel in Buckingham under the auspices of *Bachad*. Towards the end of 1946 he moved to London as a trainee accountant and graduated in December 1952.

Courtesy of Susan Lew (daughter of Sabine and Manfred Landau), London, UK

A group photo of *Kinder* who had recently arrived in England.

Courtesy of the United States Holocaust Memorial Museum

EDITH MANIKER (NÉE GRUNBAUM)

PAULA BALKIN (NÉE GRUNBAUM)

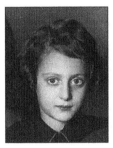

Edith was born in Leipzig, Germany, on March 12, 1931. Her sister Paula, who is seven years older, left for England in June 1939, and two weeks later, in July 1939, Edith followed. Edith went to a distant cousin of her mother's who lived in Walthamstow, a suburb of London.

On September 1, 1939, she was evacuated to a little town in Rutland, in the center of England. In December 1939 she was brought back to London and stayed there until the bombing started in June 1940, when she was evacuated to Salcombe, in the southern English county of Devon, to the home of Lady Clementine Waring. She stayed for two years until around September 1942, when she was sent back to London.

In 1943 Edith was placed in an orthodox refugee hostel and spent ten weeks there until she was reunited with Paula. They went to live with a family in Tottenham, in north London, and remained with this family until the spring of 1944, when they were 'bombed-out'. Edith and Paula found a room in nearby Stamford Hill. Paula went to work and Edith went to school. Her school was bombed, so she changed schools and then the V1 and V2 rockets started. She became very frightened so the Refugee Committee sent her to Cambridge to live in the refugee hostel. Soon after, Paula was able to join her.

When the war ended, the hostel was closed. Both sisters moved again, to an apartment in Cambridge. Here Edith finished her schooling at the Cambridgeshire Technical College and School of Art in July 1947. On July 15 Edith and Paula left England and went to Detroit, Michigan where an uncle and aunt were living.

Courtesy of Edith Maniker, Southfield, Michigan, USA

Train 16

ILONA PENNER

Ilona was born in Berlin on June 27, 1928. Her family remained together in Berlin through the early years of the Third Reich, but in March 1939 Ilona and her twin brother Kurt were sent to England on a Kindertransport for their safety.

Arrangements for their care were handled by Bloomsbury House, which placed the twins in separate homes. In 1940 their parents left Berlin, going to Belgium and France. They were interned separately by the French police before escaping to North Africa. From there, they secured safe passage to the United States in 1941. After the start of the war, Ilona was evacuated from London to Sussex. She attended a public school and later a secretarial school. Eventually, the Refugee Committee decided that Ilona should begin working. In 1941 she returned to London to work in an office. Her brother Kurt immigrated to the United States in 1943, and a few months later, in October 1943, Ilona also immigrated and was reunited with her family in Brooklyn, New York.

United States Holocaust Memorial Museum, courtesy of Ilona Penner

GROUP OF GERMAN JEWISH CHILDREN

A group of German Jewish children in an orphanage in Belgium,
where they were sent on a Kindertransport.

United States Holocaust Memorial Museum, courtesy of Hans and Ilse Garfunkel

FRIEDA STOLZBERG KOROBKIN

Frieda was born in Vienna into an Orthodox rabbinical family. In 1938 Frieda's parents sent her and her siblings from Austria to England on a Kindertransport. Frieda was six years old.

Vienna, Upper Belvedere

Courtesy of Frieda Korobkin, Beverly Hills, California, USA

JOSEPH GARTEN

CELIA GLUCK (NÉE GARTEN)

Joseph was born in Berlin in July 1931. His sister Celia was born in Berlin in January 1926. In December 1938 they both left on a Kindertransport, crossing the border to Holland. Since the children could not leave all at once to go to England, they stayed temporarily in a camp in Holland. Joseph arrived in England in April 1939 and Celia arrived in June the same year. They were evacuated from London to Chelmsford right after the war began and lived with a non-Jewish family for four years. Joseph and Celia were treated with great kindness and in spite of the years, they have all remained in close contact. In 1949 Joseph immigrated to the United States. He married Beatrice Schreiber and they reside in Roslyn, New York. Celia settled in England and married Leslie Gluck.

Joseph and his sister Celia

Courtesy of Joseph Garten, Roslyn, New York, USA

94

RUTH PESCHEL

Ruth Gertrude (Sara) Peschel was born in Jauer, in the Silesia region of what is now Poland, in 1923. She was the daughter of Otto Peschel, a shoemaker, and his wife Helene. Due to Nazi legislation, Ruth had to leave school in early 1937 and was unable to train as a seamstress. In 1938 she moved with her parents to Breslau, Germany.

Ruth left on a Kindertransport to England in June 1939. From Harwich, she was taken to Scotland, where she stayed at Whittingehame House in East Lothian, which was converted into a school for refugee children. The school, known as the Whittingehame Farm School, sheltered 160 children. In November 1940 she managed to get a job in a household in Leeds.

Her brother Emanuel Karl Isidor Peschel (born 1921) was deported to Auschwitz. It is not clear from the records whether he survived. Ruth's parents and her grandmother, Rosalin Grunbaum, survived the Holocaust.

Courtesy of The Wiener Library for the
Study of the Holocaust & Genocide, London, UK

Ruth was born in Berlin in 1923. Her father's family had lived in Berlin for generations. Her mother's family came from Soldin, near Poznan, Poland. In 1934 Ruth was forced to leave her mixed German and Jewish school and move to an all-Jewish middle school.

In 1939 her parents Werner and Frieda (Friedl) decided to send her and her older sister Steffi to England on a Kindertransport. Steffi left first; she barely made it, as she was just under the Kindertransport's upper age limit of 18. Ruth left on the second-to-last transport on August 10, 1939. Her sponsor was Frau Landsmann, a non-Jewish German woman who, together with Mrs. Atkinson of Dorset, helped many Jewish children find refuge.

After Ruth's arrival in England, Mrs. Atkinson, now Ruth's guarantor, sent her to a small town in Buxted, Sussex, to train for a career in nursing. She first was given the position of a trainee to a matron in a boarding school. Ruth was very unhappy there and eventually moved to a different school in Warminster, Wiltshire, where there were other refugee children. After Ruth became ill, she had to move to a new position. Since her sister was then in Birmingham, Mrs. Atkinson found her work nearby assisting mentally handicapped children.

Ruth and her husband Karl Terner

Ruth eventually convinced Mrs. Atkinson that she had no interest in that type of work and following a two-week vacation in Dorset at Mrs. Atkinson's home and farm, Ruth went to work for the war effort. While in Birmingham, Ruth met Karl Terner, a chemist and Jewish émigré from Vienna. They married in the Central Synagogue in Birmingham in 1945 and immigrated to the United States ten years later.

United States Holocaust Memorial Museum, courtesy of Ruth Hilde Terner

Ursula was born in Reichenbach, west of Breslau, in Germany. She was just three-and-a-half years old when she left on a Kindertransport out of Berlin via Breslau. She was one of the youngest on the train. She joined the ship *The Washington* in Hamburg, which docked in Southampton on its way to the United States. Ursula was met in Southampton by her uncle, who had immigrated to England in 1933. At that time, her name was Ursula Kantorowicz. Three months after her arrival, her parents were fortunate enough to obtain a visa. Her father was then interned on the Isle of Man (a small island in the Irish Sea) as a foreign alien. In 1945 he legally changed the family name to Kanter.

This document of identity is issued with the approval of His Majesty's Government in the United Kingdom to young persons to be admitted to the United Kingdom for educational purposes under the care of the Inter-Aid Committee for children.

THIS DOCUMENT REQUIRES NO VISA

PERSONAL PARTICULARS.

Name KANTOROWICZ___URSULA INGEBORG SARA

Sex FEMALE. Date of Birth 16.3.35

Place BRESLAU

Full Names and Address of Parents

KANTOROWICZ DR.FRANZ ISRAEL ~ EDITH SARA
SCHWEIDNITZERSTR.
REICHENBACH
EULENGEB.

Courtesy of Ursula Ader, London, UK

Train Seventeen

97

Ilse was born on December 25, 1925, in Stettin, Germany. Throughout the 1930s, Ilse faced growing anti-Semitic harassment from her classmates at the local public elementary school until she was finally expelled in 1936 and forced to attend the Jewish school. Shortly after Kristallnacht, Ilse's parents sent her on a Kindertransport to Belgium. She left in January 1939 and three months later her parents left for Shanghai.

Following the German invasion of Belgium in May 1940, Ilse and her group of German Jewish refugees were evacuated to France. After a very difficult journey, the children finally arrived in Seyre (Haute Garonne) on May 18, 1940. They remained there for over a year, living in extremely primitive conditions.

In the spring of 1941 the Swiss Children's Aid found new accommodations for them at a home called Chateau de la Hille. For the first year the children lived in relative security. However, on August 26, 1942, the French police raided the home and rounded up some forty of the older children, including Ilse. They were taken to Le Vernet internment camp to await deportation. In the meantime, Rosali Naef, the director of La Hille, contacted the local head of the Secours Suisse, who went to Marseilles to plead for the release of the children. He was successful, and the children returned to La Hille in September. The situation remained too dangerous for the teenagers to remain there, so individually and in groups they were smuggled over the border into Switzerland on the night of December 31, 1942.

After spending time in two refugee camps, Ilse was placed in the home of a Protestant minister, Pastor Charles Brutsch. The minister treated Ilse as a member of his family. She lived with them for two years while she studied pediatric nursing. Ilse remained in contact with the Brutsch family after the war.

United States Holocaust Memorial Museum,
courtesy of Hans and Ilse Garfunkel

Ilse was born on February 24, 1923, in Volkmarsen, a town of about 6000 people in central Germany. She had an older brother, Arthur, born on May 7, 1920, and a younger sister, Inge, born on February 4, 1930. The children attended the local public Catholic school and also received Jewish education one afternoon a week. Their father read the *Torah* in the town's synagogue and gave his children extra Jewish education on Saturday afternoons.

In May 1938 Arthur left Germany and immigrated to America. The rest of the family hoped to immigrate as well. On January 4, 1939, Ilse and Inge joined a Kindertransport that left nearby Kassel for Holland. The trip took twelve hours, and as the oldest member of the transport, Ilse helped care for the younger children. After initial processing, Ilse and Inge went to a camp in Bergen aan Zee, a town on the North Sea Coast in the Dutch Province of North Holland, where they stayed for three months. The group was later moved close to Rotterdam. Inge stayed together with Ilse until September 1939, when Inge was sent to live with a Jewish foster family in Blydorp, a suburb of Rotterdam. Meanwhile, Arthur tried to secure affidavits to bring the family to the United States. He succeeded in sending one to Ilse, but was unable to secure visas for the rest of the family.

Arthur enlisted in the US Army in August 1941 and spent the war serving in the Aleutian Islands. Isle left Holland on April 4, 1940, on board the cruise ship *MS Volendam* and arrived in New York on April 16. The following month Germany invaded Holland. Inge's foster parents decided that it was no longer safe to keep her and sent her home to her parents in Volkmarsen. No longer permitted to attend German public school, Inge commuted daily to Kassel to attend the Jewish school. Inge and her parents were later deported June 1, 1942, to Sobibor and were murdered very soon after their arrival. Once in the United States, Ilse met a childhood friend, Meinhard Meyer. In June 1943 Meinhard was drafted into the US Army and sent to the Pacific theater of Operations. He returned home in February 1945. Ilse and Meinhard married in 1955.

United States Holocaust Memorial Museum,
courtesy of Ilse (Lichtenstein) Meyer

Train Seventeen

Train 18

RUTH SEGAL (NÉE WASSERMANN)

Ruth was born May 20, 1926, in Nuremberg, Germany. Her older sister, Anneliese, was born in 1921. In the spring of 1933 her father's health began to deteriorate due to tuberculosis. At the same time, his business began to suffer because of the anti-Jewish boycott. To make ends meet, the family was forced to rent out their home and move to an apartment. In 1935 they were forced to liquidate their business and two years later, in April 1937, they moved to Berlin.

After Kristallnacht, the family focused all their efforts on getting their two girls out of Germany. The Wassermans had a cousin in London affiliated with the B'nai B'rith organization, who was able to get both girls on a Kindertransport. Ruth and Anneliese arrived in England on April 8, 1939, and were taken to Bloomsbury House in London. Immediately upon their arrival, the sisters were separated. Anneliese was assigned domestic work while Ruth was sent to live with a foster family. Later, she was transferred to a B'nai B'rith youth hostel in Hackney, London.

In September 1939 all the children from the hostel were evacuated to Cockley Cley in Norfolk, where Ruth remained until August 1941, when she was sent back to London to work. She once again lived in a B'nai B'rith hostel. Meanwhile, Ruth and Anneliese's parents succeeded in leaving Germany in July 1940. They traveled the Trans-Siberian railroad to the city of Vladivostok, in the Russian Far East. From there they made their way to Kobe, Japan. They remained in Kobe for three weeks until they were able to secure safe passage on a Japanese freighter sailing from Yokohama to South America. After seven weeks at sea, they disembarked in Panama in September 1940. Sadly, their father's health had deteriorated and he died in December 1940. In February 1941 their mother immigrated to the United States, which is where, after the war, she was reunited with both her girls.

Nuremberg, Germany

United States Holocaust Memorial Museum, courtesy of Ruth Wasserman

EMMANUEL ZINGER

MARCUS ZINGER

Emmanuel and Marcus at a training farm and school in Scotland that provided shelter for German and Austrian Jewish youth who came on the Kindertransports.

Courtesy of the United States Holocaust Memorial Museum

JOSZI ROSENZWEIG

GUNTHER ABRAHAMSON

HANS SILBERSTEIN

Joszi Rosenzweig from Vienna, Gunther Abrahamson from Berlin and Hans Silberstein from Danzig in the Priory, a children's home in Selkirk, Scotland. The assistant matron in the Priory was Netta Pringle, who formed warm relations with many of the Jewish children.

United States Holocaust Memorial Museum, courtesy of Gunther Abrahamson

TWO REFUGEE CHILDREN

The boy with an identification tag is Peter Laufer, then aged five or six years old. He traveled from Vienna and arrived in Britain on December 12, 1938. He eventually settled in Miami, Florida.

Courtesy of The Wiener Library for the Study of the Holocaust & Genocide, London, UK

THEO ENGELHARD

Theo was born in 1927 in Munich. He had two sisters: Bertha, who was born in 1923, and Inge, who was born in January, 1930. All three siblings attended a Jewish school in Munich from September 1936 until it closed in November 1938. After Kristallnacht, the children attended makeshift schools and all were registered for the Kindertransport to England. Bertha and Theo departed in January 1939 and Inge was put on a waiting list for a later transport.

United States Holocaust Memorial Museum, courtesy of Inge Engelhard Sadan

JO LEHMANN

Jo Lehmann was one of a number of German Jewish refugee children who went to Australia on the *SS Orama*.

United States Holocaust Memorial Museum, courtesy of Dr. Glen Palmer

FANNY KOPFSTEIN (NÉE FLOHR)

GISA WERTHAJM (NÉE FLOHR)

Fanny and Gisa were born in Vienna. Fanny was born on May 3, 1922, and Gisa on October 28, 1923. Their mother, Sabine Schachner, died in 1937 in her thirties, soon after the tragic death of their five-year-old brother from undiagnosed diphtheria.

Gisa (left) and Fanny with their father Gershon.

The day war broke out, Gwrych Castle.

Organized by Bnei Akiva and Arieh Handler as part of the Kindertransport during World War II, hundreds of Jewish children were given refuge at Gwrych Castle. The facilities were extremely basic, with no running water or electricity, as the castle was not connected to the main water and electricity supplies, and no fuel was available for the generators. The children left Gwrych only after the war had ended.

Before deciding to send his daughters on a Kindertransport, their father Gershon went with them to ask the Chortkover Rebbe what to do. The Chortkover Rebbe came from a very wealthy dynasty and lived in a palace outside Vienna and saw them in what appeared to be a stateroom. Fanny recalled walking backwards and bowing all the way until they reached the door. The Rebbe spoke just two words: '*Heraus heraus!*' (send them away). On the basis of that, Gershon, unlike other Chassidim, allowed his daughters to go on the Kindertransport, having been awaiting affidavits to send them to family in New York, hoping that he would follow.

The sisters left Vienna separately in July/August 1939. Fanny did not travel with Gisa because she had been arrested in Vienna for defying a Nazi officer by refusing to step aside from the pavement into the road to let him pass. The police came to their flat in the middle of the night and took her to prison. She remained there for three weeks until she was released on condition that she left the country within hours. On both occasions when their father accompanied them to the station to wave them goodbye, it was to be the last time they saw each other. He was taken to Buchenwald in October 1939 and died of a heart attack in March 1940, aged 44.

On arrival in England, both sisters went to Ashford, Kent, and from there to Gwrych Castle in Wales. The castle became home to some 300 youngsters, with Arieh Handler and his brother Dr. Handler in charge, and Rabbi Sperber responsible for their Jewish education and spiritual needs. The youngsters had to clean the derelict castle and make it fit for use. Gisa worked in the hospital wing, aiding Dr. Handler, as she wanted to be a nurse. Fanny was assigned to the laundry, but managed to switch to the kitchen. All the young people attended the wedding of Arieh Handler to Henny Prilutsky in 1940 and both girls played the violin as the couple walked down the imposing castle staircase.

Fanny married Alec Kopfstein in 1944. They had a daughter Sylvia, named after Fanny's late mother, and a son Gershon, named after her father. Sylvia has two children and eight grandchildren. Gershon has nine children and eleven grandchildren. Gisa married Sam Werthajm in 1947. They had two daughters, Helen and Ruth, named after Sam's mother and the youngest of his five sisters who perished in the Holocaust. Helen has one son and Ruth has two sons and two grandsons. Gisa passed away in 1991 and Fanny in 2000, but their legacy lives on in their families.

Courtesy of Sylvia Barnett, Gershon Kopfstein,
Helen Bender and Ruth Lebens, London, UK

Ursula was born in January 1926 in Görlitz, Germany. In 1936, due to the increasing anti-Semitism in the local schools, Ursula's family moved to Berlin, where she began attending the Jewish Holdheim School. During Kristallnacht, Ursula's father went into hiding and her mother was very worried about the situation. She immediately made inquiries regarding safe passage for Ursula out of Germany. She contacted a cousin in England who had become a Quaker. With the cousin's help, Ursula was able to leave on a Kindertransport to England in July 1939. Ursula first lived with her cousin in Yorkshire and then stayed with her sponsor family for seven-to-eight years until she was twenty years old. Ursula's parents managed to escape to the United States in 1941 under the sponsorship of relatives in Indiana. In July 1946 Ursula also immigrated to the United States on board the *SS Gripsholm*, a Swedish American Line.

Görlitz, Germany

United States Holocaust Memorial Museum, courtesy of Ursula Meyer

Train 20

RUTH ROSENBLATT

Ruth left Germany on a Kindertransport and went to a children's home in Zuen (Brabant), Belgium.

United States Holocaust Memorial Museum, courtesy of Walter Reed

STEVE WACHSNER (FORMERLY EGON WACHSNER)

Steve (Egon) arrived in England in the spring of 1939. He was fifteen years old.

Courtesy of Steve Wachsner, Sherman Oaks, California, USA

ARNO MARCUSE

Arno left Germany on a Kindertransport in the spring of 1939 and was sent to the Quincy-sous-Senart children's home near Paris.

Courtesy of the United States Holocaust Memorial Museum

KURT STERN

Kurt was born in April 1929 in Chodov, Czechoslovakia. Kurt's mother Erna Stern (née Kronberger) registered him for the Winton Kindertransport and Kurt left for England arriving at Liverpool Street Station on June 2, 1939. Kurt was fostered with an English family, Mr. and Mrs. Nunn, in the east of England.

Today Kurt and his wife Aliza live in Israel. They have two children and five grandchildren. He will always be grateful to 'Nicky' (Sir Nicholas Winton) for saving him and 668 other children from Czechoslovakia.

Kurt aged six, sitting on his grandfather's knee, May 1935.   Kurt aged eight

Courtesy of Kurt Stern, Ramat Hasharon, Israel

Alisa (Liesl) was born in September 1929 in Vienna. Her father owned a wholesale grocery store. After Kristallnacht, the family store was confiscated by the Nazis and her father Moshe was arrested and taken to Dachau. However, on January 27, 1939, he was released from the camp on condition that he would leave Austria. Fortunately, he was able to join a group of men who were leaving for Great Britain and he left on April 13, 1939. Once in Britain, he tried his best to bring his family to him. Though unable to find a job for his wife, he nevertheless managed to arrange for Alisa to come on the last Kindertransport from Vienna to England.

Organized by the Newcastle Jewish Community, the Kindertransport left in August 1939. Alisa was taken to Percy Park in Tynemouth, where she stayed in a hostel until May/June 1940. She then lived in another hostel for Jewish girls in Windermere until the end of the war. Alisa's sister, who was seven years older than her, left in January 1939 with the Youth Aliyah to Palestine.

Meanwhile, Alisa's father joined the Pioneer Corps. Alisa's mother, all alone in Vienna, was deported to the Lodz Ghetto. From there, she was sent to Auschwitz – the Krupp ammunition factory (forced labor) – from there to Sachsenhausen, and then to Ravensbrück, where she was liberated. After recuperating in Sweden, Alisa's mother and her family were reunited and left Glasgow, Scotland in October 1949. They spent a few days in London with friends and then went by train to Marseilles, where they boarded the freight ship *Kedma* as new immigrants bound for Palestine.

Alisa is fluent in three languages: English, German and Hebrew. For the past forty years, she has talked in schools and colleges in and around Israel and Europe about the *Anschluss* and Kristallnacht, which led to the formation of the Kindertransport operation.

Alisa is the head of the Kindertransport Association in Israel and has held this position since 2000. Her husband Benjamin was the fifth generation of his family to be born in Jerusalem. She has two daughters, six grandchildren and four great-grandchildren.

Courtesy of Alisa Tennenbaum, Bet Cherut, Israel

Train Twenty

Greta was born in Bocholt, Germany, on November 4, 1924. In 1938, after Kristallnacht, her parents arranged to send her and her younger sister Ilsa (who was 11 ½) to England on a Kindertransport. They left in July 1939. Greta remembers her father taking her and Ilsa to the train station. Her mother did not go with them. Greta and Ilsa arrived at Harwich on July 7, 1939, and then continued their journey by train to London. They were separated in Cambridge: Greta stayed with a family in Cambridge and Ilsa was placed in a boarding school.

Greta (left), Jack (her older brother), and Ilsa (her younger sister), spring 1938

Ilsa and Greta (right), spring 1937

Ilsa and Greta (right), 1939

Greta married Harry Meier in England. Their families knew each other because they were both from Bocholt. In 1936 Harry's family moved from Bocholt to Frankfurt, believing things would be better in a larger city. Following Kristallnacht Harry's father was arrested and sent to Buchenwald. Eventually his mother obtained visas and managed to get Harry's father and the family out safely, and they left for England. A few months later in 1940, Harry's family settled in Baltimore, Maryland. Shortly after Greta and Harry married, Harry returned to Germany as an American soldier. Greta remained in England for a short time and then moved to Baltimore where she was reunited with Harry and his family.

Greta has four children: Carolyn, Ron, Leslie and Debbie. She also has six grandchildren and four great-grandchildren.

Courtesy of Greta Meier, West Hartford, Connecticut
(previously of Baltimore, Maryland), USA

Train 21

JOSEF HIRSCHHORN

SONIA HIRSCHHORN

Josef (Joe) was born on January 1, 1927, and Sonia was born on June 4, 1929, in Leipzig, Germany. They left on a Kindertransport to England with their elder sister Rosa. Joe married in London and later immigrated to the United States. He now lives in Florida. He has two sons and six grandchildren. Sonia married and lived in London. She had two sons and three grandchildren. She died several years ago.

Courtesy of Shirley Kenley, London, UK

GROUP OF KINDER

A group of four young German Jewish refugee boys in Great Chesterford, a village in Essex, southeast England. The boys had arrived together on a Kindertransport.

United States Holocaust Memorial Museum, courtesy of Gilda Moss Haber

ROSA SCHUSHEIM (NÉE HIRSCHHORN)

Rosa was born in Leipzig, Germany, on February 17, 1923. She was the eldest of three children. In July 1939 she left Germany on a Kindertransport with her brother Josef, aged twelve, and sister Sonia, aged ten. When they arrived in London, the siblings were separated. Rosa stayed with a family who had left Leipzig earlier. Josef and Sonia were sent to a hostel, as they were so young.

During the war their parents were in hiding in Reggiolo, Italy. Towards the end of the war, they were caught by the Germans and sent to Auschwitz where they both died.

In July 1943 Rosa married Ruben Schusheim. Rosa and Ruben had two children, Michael and Shirley, six grandchildren and eighteen great-grandchildren. Rosa died on August 18, 2012.

Courtesy of Shirley Kenley, London, UK

RUBEN SCHUSHEIM

Ruben was born on November 25, 1922, in Berlin. He was one of five children. In 1936 his two sisters and younger brother went to Palestine. Ruben left by himself on a Kindertransport to England on August 23, 1939. He stayed in a hostel in Willesden with other young people. His eldest brother, Usher Salke, remained in Europe and was arrested in Paris at the outbreak of war. He was sent to Drancy, a transit camp for Auschwitz. He was later sent to Bergen-Belsen. He survived the war and immigrated to Canada. During the war, Ruben's parents were in hiding in Lyon, France. They survived, and after the war they came to London.

Ruben met Rosa Hirschhorn in London and they married in July 1943. Ruben died on December 7, 2010.

Courtesy of Shirley Kenley, London, UK

Train 22

HOWARD 'HORST' TICHAUER

Howard was born in Germany. From 1928 until 1939 he lived in Cosel, Germany. His parents, Max and Martha Tichauer, ran a wholesale-retail confectionary shop. Because of the boycott, the shop closed and for financial reasons, the family was forced to move to the bottom floor of a community house. After Kristallnacht, Howard's father was arrested and kept in Buchenwald for about a month. He was released on the basis that he was a decorated World War I veteran. Despite his imprisonment and all the hardships, he was convinced that the Jews would not come to harm.

A wealthy cousin had gone to London to work as a governess and she sought assistance for her Tichauer relatives from Mrs. Goldsmith of the West London Synagogue. The synagogue agreed to sponsor

110 children to come to England as part of the Kindertransport. Mrs. Goldsmith arranged for Horst and his sister Erika, as well as the brother of the cousin who was already in London working as a governess, to be included on the list. Their father Max took them to Breslau to say goodbye to their older brother, Harry (Heinz). They continued on to Berlin, where they joined the other Kindertransport children and from there they sailed to Holland and finally to England, where they went to the Lingfield School in Surrey.

Their parents were sent to Theresienstadt in November 1943. Soon after, they were deported to Auschwitz, where they perished.

Courtesy of the United States Holocaust Memorial Museum

ERICA ROSENTHAL (NÉE ERIKA TICHAUER)

Erica was born in August 1926 in Bernstadt, Germany. From 1928 until 1939 she lived in Cosel, Germany, where her parents ran a wholesale-retail confectionary shop. She had two siblings: her brother Heinz, the eldest, and a younger brother Horst. She attended school, vacationed with her family, played with her brothers and friends. Those were the happy times.

During Kristallnacht, Erica and her mother were tormented by an angry mob and forced to witness the burning of their synagogue. Her father was arrested along with all the other Jewish men of Cosel. Fortunately a few weeks later he was released. But it was all very clear that they were in immediate danger. Erica's parents made arrangements with the assistance of a cousin, Ruth, who had already departed Germany for England, for her and her younger brother Horst to leave Germany on a Kindertransport. Her older brother, Heinz was too old to participate in the Kindertransport program.

August 12, 1927,
Erica's first birthday

In May 1939 she and Horst left for England on a Kindertransport. There they lived with a foster family, attended school and she later trained as a nurse. In Germany, her older brother Heinz was arrested and sent to Auschwitz. He was fortunate to survive years of slave labor. Tragically, her parents were murdered in the gas chambers of Auschwitz-Birkenau.

In 1947 she and Horst traveled to the United States and settled in New York. They were reunited with Heinz who was already there. This is where Horst became Howard, Heinz became Harry and Erika became Erica. They found housing and Erica worked in a number of hospitals. She met her future husband, Manfred, in 1950. He was introduced to her by a fellow nurse, Ruth Lebram Knopp, also a Holocaust survivor, who became a life-long friend. Erica and Manfred were married January 27, 1952, and had three sons and are

Cosel, Germany

now grandparents of six. Tragically their son Herbert died of natural causes while celebrating his 25th wedding anniversary in Africa. He left Erica and Manfred with a wonderful daughter-in-law and two granddaughters.

Erica became involved with the Center for Holocaust, Human Rights & Genocide Education at Brookdale Community College, serving as the coordinator of volunteers for twenty years. She has spoken to school groups and religious institutions as well as at the New Jersey Statehouse during a Kristallnacht memorial program.

Courtesy of the Center for Holocaust, Human Rights
& Genocide Education Center at Brookdale Community College

Hanus Jiri Grosz was born in Brno, Czechoslovakia, in February 1924 and his brother Karel was born in 1925. When the German armies invaded their home town in March 1939, their parents decided to send Hanus and Karel on a Kindertransport to England. Their mother Irma (née Meth) took the boys to Prague, while their father Emil decided to say his goodbyes in Brno.

On April 19, 1939, they assembled at the railway station in Prague, along with children of all ages up to seventeen. All waiting in anticipation with labels tied around their necks. The goodbyes were said and they boarded the train, never to see their parents and countless family members again. Dr. Emil Grosz died in Terezin and Irma Grosz was gassed in Auschwitz. Upon arriving in England, both boys were placed on a farm in a small village called Warborough, near Shillingford in Oxfordshire. Their guarantor, Lilian Bowes-Lyon, the Queen Mother's first cousin, arranged for them to work on the farm and also to receive English lessons twice a week.

When these photos were taken at Warborough, Hanus was fifteen and Karel was fourteen. The two brothers knew little English and were lonely and isolated in the countryside. After a few months Lilian Bowes-Lyon was able to arrange a placement at the Youth Aliyah training camp at the Great Engeham farm (*Hachshara*) in Kent, and eventually at another *Hachshara*, Bydown near Swimbridge in Devon, until 1941. Later Hanus joined the Royal Air Force and Karel joined the British Army. When the war ended, Hanus trained in Cardiff, Wales, to become a doctor and eventually went on to become a psychiatrist and a neurologist, continuing the family tradition of practicing medicine. Hanus immigrated to the United States in 1962, while Karel remained in England.

Courtesy of Kirsten Grosz, Sarasota, Florida/Indianapolis, Indiana, USA

REFUGEE GIRL

A refugee girl shortly after her arrival at Harwich, England, December 2, 1938, on a Kindertransport.

United States Holocaust Memorial Museum, courtesy of Bibliotheque de la Ville de Paris

RUTH KORNER

Ruth left Vienna for England on a Kindertransport in 1939.

Courtesy of Abraham (Abe) Sommer,
Los Angeles, California, USA

GERTRUDE KAHN (NÉE WOLFF)

Gertrude was born April 1925 in Neustadt/ Weinstrasse, Germany. Shortly after Kristallnacht in November 1938 she was put on one of the Kindertransports to England, where she lived through the London Blitz. Her parents eventually escaped and the family reunited in America. Gertrude currently resides in Dayton, Ohio.

Courtesy of Gertrude Kahn, Dayton, Ohio, USA

GRETE KORNER

Grete was born in Vienna in 1923. She arrived in England on a Kindertransport from Vienna in 1939. She left England for Palestine, where she met and married her husband, a *kind* from Vienna. They had two children, Ilana and Gerry. In 1957 they moved to Los Angeles. Sadly, she passed away in 1990.

Courtesy of Abraham (Abe) Sommer, Los Angeles, California, USA

ROSE WINTERNITZ

EMMA WINTERNITZ

In July 1939 Rose and her sister Emma left Vienna on a Kindertransport to England.

Courtesy of David Hassin,
Portland, Oregon, USA

ALIX GRAPKOVITZ

Alix was one of a large group of German Jewish children who arrived in Belgium on a Kindertransport and were sent to an orphanage.

*United States Holocaust Memorial Museum,
courtesy of Hans and Ilse Garfunkel*

EVA TAUSSIG

Eva was born in Prague. After her arrival in England on a Kindertransport, she was sent to the Stoatley Rough Boarding School.

The Stoatley Rough Boarding School was founded in 1934, largely through the efforts of Bertha Bracy, a Quaker, who was anxious to help the plight of German refugees. It was a mixed boarding school and catered mainly for refugee Jewish children from Nazi Europe.

United States Holocaust Memorial Museum, courtesy of Bernard Kelly

RUTH KLAHR

Ruth was born in Berlin in 1927. She arrived in England in June 1939 on a Kindertransport. In 1943 she joined the *Hachshara* group at Courthouse Kempsey in Worcestershire. She left for Los Angeles in 1947 to be with her parents who had survived Theresienstadt. In 1949 she went to Israel to Kibbutz Maayin Zvi, near Zichron Yaacov, where she met and married her husband, Hans Ehrmann. They lived on this kibbutz for thirty-eight years. Sadly, Hans passed away in 1989.

Text courtesy of Abraham (Abe) Sommer, Los Angeles, California, USA

Marion was born in Prague in 1929 into a family that was Jewish but not religiously observant. Her father also had his roots in Prague, having been born and raised there, along with three brothers and two sisters. Her mother was originally German, and grew up in Berlin. Her father was Jewish, her mother Protestant.

They lived in the part of Prague called Letna, on the fourth floor of a small apartment building at Ovenecka 42, a block away from one of the gates leading into Stromovka and so among her earliest memories are walks in the park, feeding birds, ducks and squirrels.

Her paternal grandparents were no longer alive when she was born, but she and her parents had regular contact with members of her father's family, who all lived in Prague.

Marion's father had an art gallery in which he regularly arranged exhibitions of contemporary art as well as old masters.

Her parents had both grown up in cities, but they were enthusiastic about nature and the outdoors and they regularly went on vacations: to ski in the winter and hike in the summer. One place she remembers visiting in winter was Špindlerův Mlýn, where she learned to ski.

When Marion was six years old, her parents enrolled her in their local elementary school, U Studanky, which she attended until they were forced to flee Prague in 1939. She remembers the atmosphere of apprehension that was palpable during the Spanish Civil War and the rise of Hitler in Germany. Marion's mother's parents lived in Germany and saw what was happening from closer range. They urged her mother to talk to her father about the possibility of leaving the country. Her father was reluctant, probably because he knew it might not be possible to get the rest of his family, his brothers and sisters, out as well. In the end, her mother prevailed and her father was persuaded to leave. Marion and her mother stayed behind, since Marion had no visa, and witnessed the invasion on March 15, 1939. Marion was lucky to get on to one of the Kindertransports arranged by Sir Nicholas Winton, and once she was out, her mother was able to leave as well.

Her parents entered the US on a visitor's visa. The Kindertransport brought Marion to England, where she was welcomed by her mother's sister and her son, Achim, who had emigrated earlier from Germany. Achim had settled in London where he found a job and an apartment, and he became her guardian while she was in England. However, she did not live with her aunt and cousin for more than a couple of months when the British government decided to evacuate children from cities like London to the country, anticipating that war was imminent.

Marion had just started school in London, where she was a subject of curiosity for the other children, as she spoke very little English. 'Say something in Czechoslovakian,' she was urged during school break in the playground. The children were then told they would be evacuated. Marion went Bedford, where she lived with Mrs. Florence Pestell and her two daughters, aged seventeen and nineteen. She lived there for more than two years, learned to speak English and attended church, not because they urged her to, but because everyone in the family went and she didn't want to be left out.

They were all issued gas masks and had to carry them with them wherever they went. A system of food rationing was introduced, and everyone was issued a ration coupon book. At night there was blackout. Mrs. Pestell had to sew some black curtains on to the windows so that no light would show potential enemy airplanes that there was a house below. Some of the men in Mrs. Pestell's family dug an air raid shelter for them at the bottom of the garden and started victory gardens to grow vegetables. Then there were some air raids, but fortunately nothing near them was hit. A wailing air raid siren would sound, usually in the middle of the night, and they would get out of their beds and go to the air raid shelter where they stayed until the 'all clear' siren sounded.

Her uncle Bedrich had also managed to escape to England with his wife, and at one point found out that the Czech Government in Exile had founded a school for Czech refugee children along the lines of a Realni Gymnasium in Czechoslovakia. The idea was that the children, who would probably want to return to Czechoslovakia after the war, would not forget Czech and would get a good education. He persuaded Marion's cousin Achim that this school would be a good idea for her, and so it was decided to send her there.

So Marion left the Pestell family, who had been very kind to her, and went to the Czech school, which was located in a farmhouse out in the country, in Whitchurch, Shropshire. The classes were conducted in Czech and included subjects such as Latin and algebra, which were not taught at the English school that she had attended in Bedford. There were many children like her, aged from about eleven to eighteen, who had left on a Kindertransport or through other means, but most of them had had to leave their parents behind. She was amongst the few lucky ones whose parents had managed to get out of Czechoslovakia.

The farmhouse in Shropshire eventually became too small for all of them and they moved to Wales, to a building that had been a hotel before the war. It was very pretty there, with rolling hills and grazing sheep.

Orloj astronomical clock, Prague

Her parents had made attempts to bring her to the US, but the war made that difficult. At one point, a ship carrying English children to Australia was hit by a torpedo, and for a while after the incident her parents stopped trying. Finally, in November 1944, Marion's headmaster Mr. Havlicek called her into his office and told her that her family had succeeded in getting a visa for her to travel to the United States and she should get ready to go to London on the first leg of the trip.

Marion's cousin accompanied her to Liverpool and introduced her to Hanna Beer, who had also gone to England on a Kindertransport and was now going to the US at the invitation of her uncle. She was nineteen years old and had agreed to act as Marion's guardian on the trip, as she was only fifteen and the steamship line did not allow minors to travel without an accompanying adult.

The trip to Halifax took about three weeks, as the war was still on and they were travelling in a convoy. The two girls then took a train to New York, where Marion was reunited with her parents.

Marion's father had started a gallery in New York, which he ran until his death in 1961. She went to high school and college in New York and spent most of her working life in publishing houses, working on the design of books and magazines. She and Hanna have stayed in contact through the years

During Marion's stay in England, she became agoraphobic and has since avoided travel. But in 1990 the Czech school had a reunion in Wales and she wanted to attend and also to see Prague again. She managed to do both and is very happy she was able to do so. Revisiting Prague and the house where she once lived was a strange, time-warp experience. The place had remained the same in many ways and yet it was different. Fifty years is a long time.

Courtesy of Marion Feigl, New York, New York, USA

ABRAHAM SOMMER

Abraham was born in Vienna in 1924. On August 26, 1939, he left on a Kindertransport to England with 140 children that was all set to depart at 6:00 p.m. The day before, on August 25, Britain and Poland signed a mutual assistance agreement, forcing Hitler to postpone the invasion for five days to September 1, 1939. Without this postponement, the borders would have been closed and the Kindertransport would not have left. These 140 children would have suffered the same fate as the 250 children on the 'Winton Train' that should have left September 1, 1939.

Abraham arrived at the Great Engeham Farm in Kent September 1, 1939 – the day Germany invaded Poland. He belonged to the *Hachshara* group and he first settled in Llandough Castle in South Wales. Then he moved to Gwrych Castle, eventually settling at Courthouse Kempsey in Worcestershire. This is where he started his apprenticeship in automotive electronics.

Abraham later joined the British Army and served for three and a half years. On the day of his discharge in June 1947, he left for Palestine via Port-de-Bouc, France and finally arrived there two weeks prior to the United Nations vote on partition. Abraham settled on Kibbutz Maayin Zvi, near Zichron Yaacov. In March 1950, while serving in the Israeli army, he met and married Grete Korner, also a *kind* from Vienna. They had two children, Ilana and Gerry. In 1957 they moved to Los Angeles, where Abraham opened his auto electrical business. He retired in 1994.

Sadly, Abraham lost Grete to lung cancer in 1990. In 1996 he married Ruth Klahr, also known as Klerchen, a *kind* from Berlin.

Text courtesy of Abraham (Abe) Sommer, Los Angeles, California, USA

Train 24

MARION MARSTON

Marion was born in East Prussia in January 1925. When she was two years old, her parents moved to Halle (Saale), Germany. After Kristallnacht, Marion's parents decided that she should join the Kindertransport. She arrived at Liverpool Street Station in March 1939. She stayed in London with a family until she was evacuated with her school when the outbreak of the war was imminent.

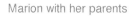
Marion with her parents

Courtesy of Marion Marston, London, UK

Ursel was the daughter of Erich and Gertrude Glasfeld. She was born in August 1924, in Berlin. Ursel left for England on one of the last Kindertransports on August 22, 1939. Her parents were subsequently deported to Theresienstadt, where her father died. Her mother perished in Auschwitz. In England, Ursel trained as a childcare worker before going on to nursing school. After the war she went to stay with an aunt in South Africa and there she met Herbert Goldschmidt, who had also come to England on a Kindertransport. A few months after his arrival, he received word from his father offering him safe passage to Johannesburg. Herbert went there from England in February 1939. He and Ursel were married in 1951.

Great Synagogue, Berlin, Germany

United States Holocaust Memorial Museum, courtesy of Herbert and Ursel Goldschmidt

Suzanne was the daughter of Max and Elsa. She was born in August 1922 in Vienna. Her brother Julius was born in 1920 and her sister Lisbeth, who was born in 1929, died in childhood. Max was a businessman. He was arrested during Kristallnacht, but soon released after producing immigration papers for the United States. Soon after, Max fled to Belgium where he remained until Germany invaded. He was arrested and deported to the French concentration camp of Gurs in 1942, but again was able to secure a release because of his American papers. Julius left Vienna for Palestine in May 1938.

Suzanne left on a Kindertransport to England June 21, 1939, and her mother left for the United States in September 1939. Suzanne spent the next eighteen months or so in Edinburgh, Aberfoyle and Selkirk, in Scotland. In January 1941 she secured safe passage on a ship to Canada. From there, she continued to New York, where she stayed with her mother and aunt. She met her husband, Otto Perl, in Brooklyn, and they married on June 20, 1943.

Vienna street scene, Austria

Courtesy of the United States Holocaust Memorial Museum

HANNA SLOME (NÉE BEER)

In May 1939, one month after her fourteenth birthday, Hanna left home on a Winton train. She grew up in Moravská Ostrava, Czechoslovakia, where her first four years of school were in a Jewish school, followed by four years in a state-run gymnasium. Her father was a successful lawyer as well as chairman of the Maccabi Sports Club. He organized skiing trips to the Tatra Mountains in Slovakia for four weeks every Christmas and Easter. They would rent the entire hotel and close to 100 members would attend. During the rest of the year, he would lead hikes every Sunday in their local Bezkydy mountains. Hanna's life was ideal.

They lived in a five-room spacious ground floor apartment with full-time live-in help. Hanna can still remember the delicious taste of some of her cook's special dishes. In addition to the cook, they hired a nanny who looked after her and her older brother John (Hans) and helped them with their homework. Hanna's mother was well educated and knew French and English. They owned a grand piano, which she frequently played very beautifully. She was always willing to help others. For example, she would have the seamstress turn their winter coats inside out and remake them for people less fortunate than them.

In 1939 Hanna's father arranged a visa for her brother to go to the USA to work at the World's Fair. Her father felt that a war would be imminent. Having nearly lost his life in World War I, he felt that wars were not the way to settle problems and did not want his son, then seventeen, to be fighting in it. John did not want to travel by himself across Germany, so the plan was for their father to accompany him until the Dutch border. On March 15, when they arrived in Germany, they found out that Czechoslovakia had been invaded by Hitler. Her father knew that as a high profile lawyer and Jewish community leader, he would be a prime target of the Nazis so they crossed the border into Holland together and arrived in England as refugees.

Hanna was on the fourth Czech Kindertransport organized by Nicholas Winton. It was difficult to leave her mother at the train station but it was made a little easier when she was asked to hold a baby girl in her arms for the beginning of the trip. She often wondered what became of this little girl. Hanna's mother helped Jews to get across the border into Poland, but she herself would not leave her sister and parents behind. She believed it would soon be over.

Assisted by the Jewish Agency, Hanna's father and brother were placed in a boarding house in Willesden Green, London. They shared two rooms with another refugee and his son from Germany. The man had lost his wife in Italy while escaping from Hitler. When Hanna arrived on the May Kindertransport, she was sent there and shared a room with his daughter. Hanna is still in contact with her. She lives in London. Hanna attended school for six weeks, fulfilling the English requirement of compulsory education, but barely understanding any English. These were not the happiest years.

Many years later, Hanna learned that her mother and grandmother had been sent briefly to Terezin and then to Treblinka, where they perished. When her father realized that no one had survived, he became very depressed and in 1949 took his own life using his gas stove.

During the war, her brother enlisted in the British Army. The army made it possible for him to attend Cambridge University, and he became a successful publisher at Heinemann Books. He spoke several languages and was awarded the MBE by Queen Elizabeth II for furthering the trade between Europe and England. At the age of sixty-five, a week before retirement, he took his own life with an overdose.

By 1943, Hanna had learned typing and stenography. When she was nineteen years old, in November 1944, she crossed the Atlantic in a large convoy of boats leaving from Liverpool and traveling for twenty-one days to get to Halifax, Nova Scotia and from there to New York. In New York she lived in a rented room for $6 a week while working as a secretary for $25 a week in Manhattan.

She tried to continue her education at Jamaica High School in Queens at night but just could not pass tests in algebra and American history in order to get her high school diploma. She fell in love with Henry, who was a friend of a friend from Ostrava. He was born in Berlin and went to high school in Lisbon. He spoke five languages. He arrived in the USA in 1940 with his parents. He enlisted in the army and was assigned to the Counterintelligence Corps, where he extracted information from German prisoners during the war. They had twenty-five unbelievably happy years together. He died in 1974.

Hanna has two children. Her son lives in Los Angeles and has three children who were brought up as Conservative Jews. Her daughter is Orthodox, lives in Israel and has four children.

Text courtesy of Hanna Slome, Flushing, New York, USA

IVAN ROSE

HENRI RETTIG

GERT ALEXANDER

SIEGFRIED KNOP

HANS STERN

Jewish refugee boys Ivan Rose, Henri Rettig, Gert Alexander, Siegfried Knop and Hans Stern came to France on a Kindertransport from Germany. These boys were taken to a chateau at Quincy-sous-Senart (about nineteen miles southeast of Paris). Quincy serviced as a Jewish children's home until September 1940, when, following the German occupation of France, the chateau was requisitioned by the German Army. The boys were then relocated to other OSE homes.

United States Holocaust Memorial Museum, courtesy of Lida Jablonski

Train 26

LILLY RADCLIFFE (NÉE HIRSCHFELD)

Lilly spent her childhood in Vienna. Following the *Anschluss* that brought about social and legal changes and then the events of Kristallnacht in November 1938, Lilly left Vienna on a Kindertransport in January 1939 and went to London and Manchester. She was thirteen. Her parents perished in Auschwitz.

One of ninety destroyed synagogues, Vienna

Courtesy of Lilly Radcliffe, Redwood City, California, USA

LORRANE DELLHEIM (NÉE GUNDELFINGER)

HELEN HARTOCH (NÉE GUNDELFINGER)

Lorrane (Lorle) was born May 18, 1928, and her younger sister Helen was born July 3, 1930, in Nuremberg, Germany. They had a very happy childhood until Kristallnacht, when their house was partly destroyed by Nazi storm troopers. Lorle and Helen's parents, Ludwig and Betty Gundelfinger, realized it was too dangerous for Jews to stay in Nuremberg, or anywhere in Germany, and made the very difficult decision to send their girls away, hoping to join them a few months later. In the spring of 1939, Lorle and Helen left on a Kindertransport to England. Four and a half years later, in October 1943, after living with very kind-hearted Jewish families, the two sisters left for the USA on the *SS Umgeni*, a freighter that sailed in a convoy.

Meanwhile, their parents, together with their grandfather Willy Wolff, were able to flee Germany in October 1940 on the Trans-Siberian Express through Russia and Siberia, and then from Japan by ship to San Francisco and finally a train to Newark, New Jersey. They began a new life and tried to get their daughters back. The family was finally reunited on October 10, 1943, a day Betty Gundell named 'Children's Day'. (The family name was changed from Gundelfinger to Gundell.)

In 1956 Helen married Kenneth Hartoch. Their son Dr. Richard Hartoch resides in Portland, Oregon, and their daughter Janice Hartoch Taylor resides in Santa Barbara, California. They have one grandchild, Samuel Alexander Hartoch, in Portland.

Lorrane married John Dellheim, who has since died. Her daughter Miriam is married to Dr. Andrew Baumel and they have four children in Massachusetts. Her son Michael has three children in New York State.

Courtesy of Helen and Ken Hartoch, Teaneck, New Jersey,
and Santa Barbara, California, USA

HERBERT GOLDSMITH (FORMERLY GOLDSCHMIDT)

Herbert was born on August 3, 1922, in Delmenhorst, northwest Germany. He arrived in England on January 19, 1939. He traveled by boat from Hamburg to Harwich. Herbert died in 1999.

Courtesy of Jennifer Weider, London, UK

CHARLES 'KARL' GOLDSMITH

(formerly Goldschmidt)

Charles was born on December 15, 1927, in Delmenhorst, northwest Germany. He arrived in England in early February 1939. He traveled by boat from Hamburg to Harwich. Charles died in 2007.

Synagogue in Delmenhorst, Germany

Courtesy of Jennifer Weider, London, UK

PAUL KUTTNER

Paul's beloved sister Annemarie was nine years old when he was born in Berlin, in September 1922. Paul was shattered when in February 1939, at the age of sixteen, he left his parents and Annemarie in Berlin, when he was placed on a Kindertransport bound for England. At the end of the 1940s Paul immigrated to the United States and lived an extraordinary life. He has authored many books. His most recent best seller, *An Endless Struggle,* is a unique 'must-read' book, written from first-hand experience.

'Kuttner demonstrates an extraordinary knowledge of the circumstances and events involved in it – so that the reader learns a great deal that is beyond the general knowledge of this sordid episode of World War II.' –Small Press Book Review

Courtesy of Paul Kuttner, Jackson Heights, New York, USA

LISL SCHICK (NÉE PORGES)

WALTER PORGES

Lisl was born in Vienna in 1927 and her brother Walter was born in 1931. Lisl was eleven and Walter just seven when they left Vienna on a Kindertransport to England. Lisl stayed in England and Wales until the war ended. Their father was able to come to England. In 1940 their mother went to New York, where she stayed briefly with relatives after having lived alone in a one-room apartment for a few years. The family was reunited in January 1945, when Lisl and her brother and father came to New York.

Courtesy of Lisl Schick, Largo, Florida, USA

Train 27

EDITH MOLLERICK

RALPH MOLLERICK

Ralph was born on May 27, 1930, in Kassel, Germany. He lived with his parents and sister Edith in the North Hessian town of Wolfhagen. In 1937 he and his family were forced to leave Wolfhagen because life for Jewish people had become increasingly difficult. The family initially sought refuge in Hamburg. A year later, on December 14, 1938, his parents sent him and Edith to safety on one of the Kindertransports to England. The photo of Ralph and Edith was taken just before they left Germany.

Courtesy of Ralph Mollerick, Lake Worth, Florida, USA

ANNE 'ANNY' KELEMEN

Anne was born in Vienna in February 1925. After a traumatic search for a sponsor, undertaken by her sister who at 18 had left Vienna to become a domestic in England, Anne left Vienna on May 13, 1939, and arrived in England two days later. The Kindertransport train crossed from Nazi Germany into Holland, and the children then left from the Hook of Holland for England, a very rough journey.

Anne clearly remembers how they were off-loaded at the railway station and to this day always thinks of it as a cattle market – with groups of children, huddled together, hoping that they were very quickly going to be identified by their sponsors or selected by the many people walking around look for a 'little blond boy' or a 'pretty dark-haired girl' they were willing to take home. In the end, just a few children remained waiting to be placed or collected. Anne was one of them until her sister arrived, breathlessly, taking her by the arm to the underground and directing her to the escalator.

This, for Anne, was a frightening experience watching these moving steps descending into the unseen depths. But there was no time to contemplate this descent into the unknown, because her sister made it clear that they had another train to catch at another railway station that would take her to Swanage, Dorset, where she would attend boarding school. In Swanage, Anne was met by one of the teachers. Swanage was a nice place by the sea, a quiet resort and a popular retirement destination for officers and families returning from service in the colonies.

Anne's parents remained in Vienna. They were deported to the East and she never saw them again. Although Anne had been told by the Red Cross, and in the years to follow by many agencies, the date when her parents had been taken to Izbica, a transit camp in Kreis Lublin, Poland, and from there most likely to Belzec extermination camp, she has never, not for one moment in the past sixty-four years, stopped looking for them and trying to piece together their last journey. In doing so, she has amassed many details about the killing camps in the East and the deportations from Vienna.

Courtesy of Anne Kelemen, New York, New York, USA

Train Twenty-Seven

ANNE 'ANNEMARIE' LEHMANN

Anne (Annemarie) was born in Germany in 1926. After Kristallnacht Anne's parents made the decision to register her for the Kindertransport and she left for England in December 1938, aged twelve.

Courtesy of the United States Holocaust Memorial Museum

GROUP OF YOUNG JEWISH REFUGEES

Young Jewish girls shortly after their arrival in England
from Dresden, Vienna and Berlin.

Courtesy of the United States Holocaust Memorial Museum

RITA WISLICKI

R ita, a young Jewish refugee girl, came to England on a Kindertransport and went to the B'nai B'rith hostel in Hackney.

United States Holocaust Memorial Museum, courtesy of Ruth Wasserman Segal

MARION EHRICH

ILSE FRANK

Marion and Ilse, both German Jewish refugee children, pictured together on the deck of the passenger liner the *SS Orama* while en route to Australia.

United States Holocaust Memorial Museum, courtesy of Dr. Glen Palmer

arry was born in December 1925 in Vienna. His parents were born in Poland and had met each other in Vienna. Harry's mother came from a religious community in Poland. His father was a real gentleman and very protective towards Harry and his sister Gerta. As a child, Harry loved ice-skating. He had learned to skate when he was five and he would spend most of his free time at the ice rink in Vienna.

Everything changed when Harry was twelve and Hitler occupied Austria. In his class, there were twelve Jewish children and about thirty-eight non-Jewish children. They were all friends until Friday, March 11, 1938. When Harry went back into school the following Monday, there was a barrier between the two groups. The non-Jewish children had clearly been told by their parents not to associate with the Jewish children. When the Jewish children started conversations, the response from the non-Jewish children was a blunt 'yes' or 'no'. Later on, Jewish children were dismissed from their grammar school.

In November 1938 Harry's father's business was destroyed during Kristallnacht. The following day, Harry's father was arrested. A few hours later, on November 10, Harry and his mother and sister were collected by the Nazi police. First, they were taken to the police headquarters and then to an apartment where there were around 25-30 Jewish women and children. They stayed there for about ten days and then they were allowed to go home. Harry's father came back as well and told them that he had been held in prison. His shop had been destroyed, all the stock had been stolen and the mirrors and fittings broken. After these terrifying events families started leaving. Harry's parents decided that they all had to emigrate, but they had no family in England or America who could help them get the right travel papers. His father told them that it would be possible to go to Shanghai and he sold all the valuables in their apartment and his mother's jewelry, but he was robbed

Harry Bibring as a young man

on his way to pay for the tickets, so Shanghai was no longer a possibility. A few days later Harry's father heard about the Kindertransport scheme and was anxious that Harry and Gerta would get a space on this transport. A family friend in England would sponsor them and his parents would find a way of joining them as soon as possible.

Harry and Gerta left Vienna in March 1939. Harry was thirteen and some of children were much younger. It was the first time they had ever been anywhere on their own.

Harry went to school in London until the outbreak of the war, when he was evacuated to the country. On his fourteenth birthday he returned to London, where he worked as a shop boy in his sponsor's clothing store. Harry corresponded with his parents until their deaths early on in the war. His father died of a heart attack on the van when they tried to take him away in November 1940. His mother then lived with her sister in lodgings until they were both deported first to Izbica and then to Sobibor in about June 1942.

Harry later moved out of his sponsor's house and found work as an engineering apprentice until the end of the war. In May 1945 Harry met his wife-to-be and they married two years later. He went to night school to become a professional engineer. During this time he and his wife had a son and today he has two gorgeous grandchildren and two great-grandsons. By 1958 Harry had two degrees and worked as an engineer. Later he taught engineering until he retired in 1993.

Courtesy of Harry Bibring, London, UK

ELSE ROSENBLATT

Else was one of three sisters who came to Belgium on a Kindertransport, part of the rescue effort organized by the *Comité d'Assistance aux Enfants Juifs Réfugiés* (CAEJR), founded by Madame Goldschmidt-Brodsky, whose husband Alfred was an official of the Belgian Red Cross. Most of the children were sheltered in private homes and about eighty were in two large children's homes. The girls' home, known as the Home General Bernheim, was located in the Brussels suburb of Zuen, and the boys' home, called Home Speyer, was located in the suburb of Anderlecht.

United States Holocaust Memorial Museum, courtesy of Walter Reed

Helga was born in Berlin in 1925. She was an only child from a middle-class family. She spent her childhood summers with an aunt in Danzig, where she first encountered anti-Semitism. Helga attended a public school until it was no longer permitted for Jewish children. Then she went to a private Jewish school. She was not allowed to go to the swimming pool nor to participate in the gymnastics display at the 1936 Olympic Games. Helga was old enough to be aware of anti-Semitism – on the streets of Berlin she saw large billboards with anti-Jewish slogans and caricatures. She remembers seeing many Nazi parades, and one in particular, where she saw Hitler standing in his Mercedes car, the people lining the streets in adoration, saluting and shouting: 'Sieg Heil.'

One morning on her way to school, she saw the broken windows of a Jewish fur store and further on a synagogue was burning. This was the beginning of Kristallnacht. That evening, Helga watched from her apartment as the pharmacy across the street was vandalized, windows smashed and shelves overturned. To this day, she can still hear all that glass breaking. In March 1939 her parents managed to get her a place on a Kindertransport to England. They were unable to obtain visas for themselves. Due to her father's severe heart condition and because his assets were frozen by the Nazi regime, it was impossible for him to find refuge in another country and her mother decided to stay with him. Helga went to a good home with a Jewish family in England – Anne and Jack Posnansky. It was, however, a completely different life. She was amongst strangers in a strange country with different customs and she spoke very little English. She made every effort to adapt to her new environment. War broke out a few months later and contact with her parents ended.

Helga found out later that her parents had been 'picked up' in their Berlin apartment and then sent to a detention center. Her father died there due to a lack of medicine. Her mother was deported to the Theresienstadt concentration camp, where she was a slave laborer in a factory. Her mother survived the severe hardships of this camp.

As much as she longed to be reunited with her mother, Helga felt torn between her German mother and her English family. It must have been very hard for her mother, who expressed how her will to survive was driven mainly by her desire to see her daughter again. Helga and her mother did eventually become close, but it was a traumatic period for both of them. This, Helga came to realize, was not uncommon with Kindertransport children.

Helga received her nursing certification in England and worked there for many years until moving to Montreal, where she worked in the operating room at the Montreal Neurological Institute. Helga and her mother moved to Los Angeles in 1962. There, she worked at the Kaiser Foundation Hospital and became a member of the original open heart surgery team. After studying at the first anesthesia program to open in southern California, she practiced in this field.

Helga met her husband John while skiing and they married in 1971. Her mother died the following year. After Helga retired, she moved to Santa Barbara, California.

Helga with her father on his 50th birthday.

Photo and text courtesy of Helga Carden, Santa Barbara, California, USA

EVA HAYMAN (NÉE DIAMANTOVA)

Eva was born in Prague in January 1924. Eva was fifteen when she and her younger sister, Vera Gissing (née Diamantova), were rescued by Nicholas Winton, who arranged safe passage for both sisters via a Kindertransport from Czechoslovakia to England. Eva attended boarding school in England for two years. After school, she went into nursing and worked as a nurse for four years. Eva married an English doctor and in 1957 they moved to New Zealand with their two children. She went to university and gained a BA and an MA with Honors and a few years later published a book entitled *By the Moon and the Stars.*

Courtesy of Eva Hayman, Auckland, New Zealand

Train 29

ERNEST GOODMAN

Ernest was born in Breslau, Germany. He left for England on a Kindertransport approximately one week before the Nazi invasion of Poland on September 1, 1939.

Courtesy of the United States Holocaust Memorial Museum

George was born in November 1931 in Berlin. He came to England on a Kindertransport in July 1939. During the Blitz he was evacuated and sent to live in a vicarage in the village of Barnack. In the meantime, his mother's brother, who had immigrated to the United States a few years earlier, tried to get George to join him there. In March 1945 George succeeded in getting transport to North America from Greenock Harbor in Scotland on a boat carrying two hundred civilians and six thousand returning Canadian soldiers. They arrived in Halifax, Canada. From there he left for Montreal, where his uncle met him and drove him to his home in New Jersey. In 1949 he and his uncle moved to Israel.

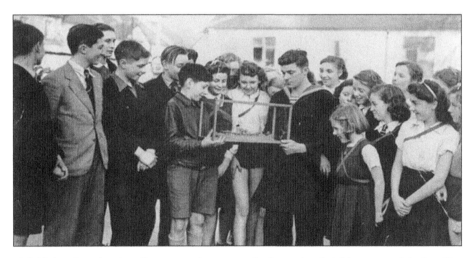

A British sailor showing George and a group of other school children a model of a ship.

United States Holocaust Memorial Museum, courtesy of George Shefi

Train 30

KARLA PILPEL (NÉE ROTHSTEIN)

Karla was born in Berlin in December 1931. She was the youngest of three children and came from a religious family. Her father had a material shop and her mother took care of her with the help of a nanny. Just before Passover in 1939 she was told that plans were being made for her and her sister to go away to England for a vacation. They left Berlin in May 1939 and crossed the border to Holland. From the Hook of Holland they went by boat to Harwich and from there by train to Liverpool Street Station. After many hours of waiting, they were collected from the

station and taken to Manchester, where Karla and her sister were separated. When the war broke out they were both evacuated to Blackpool. In 1951 Karla moved to Israel. She and her husband Abraham have two children and five grandchildren.

Courtesy of Karla Pilpel, Jerusalem, Israel

Daisy was born in Vienna on February 21, 1926, and moved to Berlin with her family in 1936. She left on a Kindertransport from Berlin in June 1939, which went to Sunderland in northern England via Holland and London.

In 1949 Daisy married Mendel Roessler, who had come from Germany via Holland to England on the last boat out of Rotterdam on May 14, 1939. They had a daughter, Susan, three grandchildren and ten great-grandchildren.

Daisy and three friends wrote *And Then There Were Four*. In 2011, shortly before she died, Daisy wrote about her experiences on the Kindertransport.

Kindertransport June 5-6, 1939
By Daisy Roessler-Rubin

On June 5, 1939, I left Berlin on a Kindertransport. Only two adults were allowed to see us off and we had to say our goodbyes in a special waiting room. The scene remains in my memory to this very day. Everyone in tears, little children grasping their mothers' skirts not understanding what was going on, older ones trying to keep a stiff upper lip, and to be brave.

I was twelve years old and was asked to look after a little girl called Lisa. The volunteers who were to accompany us to England asked most of us 'older ones' to assist with the younger travelers, some of whom were only four years old!

We had identification cards round our necks with our name and destination, and we were allowed one medium-sized suitcase and a small bag.

There were lots of people waiting at the Dutch border. They shouted 'welcome' and handed us food and drinks, as well as toys for the younger children. Then on to the Hook of Holland for the next phase of our long, long journey. Most of us had never seen the sea before, so our misery was somewhat alleviated by the view. We boarded the ferry, we were assigned our berths, served a warm meal, and off we went to sleep after a long, sad and eventful day.

On the morning of June 6 we disembarked and stepped on to British soil. It was a lovely day. We boarded a train which took us to Liverpool Street station. A new identification card with name and destination was placed around my neck. I was put in charge of two smaller girls, and we were each handed a ten shilling note. It was a lot of money in those days – about a fifth of a working man's weekly wage.

We then boarded another train at Kings Cross station, which I was later told was the renowned Flying Scotsman. We were put under the charge of the guard who sat us down in the dining car. This was the first time I heard the word 'refugee', when he explained who we were to the other passengers. The two girls soon nodded off leaning on my shoulders. Everyone smiled at us and ordered food and drink for us. I knew no English, so all I could do was smile back.

Our destination turned out to be Newcastle, where we were met by two ladies, driven to Sunderland, and reached what was to be our new home: 2 Kensington Esplanade, a four-story double-fronted upper middle-class Victorian mansion.

Miss Schlüssel the matron, Miss Rosenberg the cook, and Rose and Maud the maids waited to receive us and show us to our rooms. After a bath and snack they sent us straight to bed. We were mostly six girls to a room with each girl having separate cupboard space

The house had three large reception rooms, a butler's pantry, the housekeeper's sitting-room with a coal-fired Aga oven, pulleys over-head to dry the laundry, and dressers along one wall for plates, cups and bowls, etc. Next door there was a kitchen with sinks, gas cooker and a long wooden table. As usual in those old houses, there was just one small coal fireplace. It was always cold – even in the summer.

At first all but the youngest girls went to the local schools, but they left after two weeks as the committee decided that the priority should be English lessons. The committee hired Miss Robinson, a most wonderful, kind and delightful retired teacher, who came each day. She really cared for us. She gave every girl a photo album for her birthday with a loving greeting on the front page.

The postman's arrival was an eagerly awaited event. He would arrive waving a handful of letters from afar.

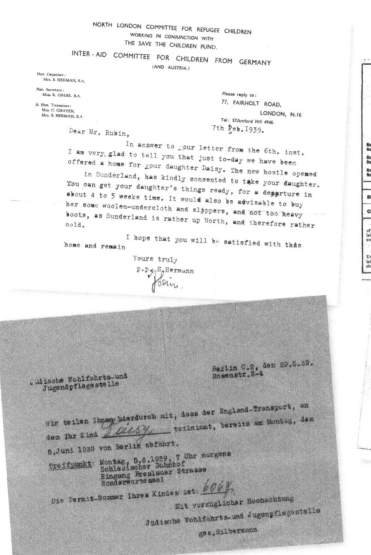

Permit number

Sunderland had two synagogues – Rabbi Rabinowitz was the minister of the Federation, and Rabbi Toporoff of the United. On Shabbat we alternated between the two, and small groups of girls would be invited for tea by some of the congregants. We were looked after by the Jewish doctors and dentists, received clothes and shoes from the local shopkeepers, and were treated well by all.

The summer of 1939 was hot and sunny. We went to the beach crocodile fashion, two by two. People would stop us with good wishes, money for ice-cream and even cinema tickets. But then came the big change! It was midday on Sunday, September 3, 1939, that Matron asked us to assemble in the playroom, sit quietly on the floor, and listen.

I remember Mr. Chamberlain declaring war without understanding most of his speech. Immediately afterwards the air-raid siren wailed for the first time. We took our gas masks off our numbered towel hooks and, together with our most valued possessions, proceeded down into the cellar which served as an air-raid shelter.

The cellar consisted of three parts: coal, general storage and wine. We sat on the side of the empty wine shelves clutching our bags. After the 'all-clear' we climbed out again.

As the war progressed, the air-raid wardens came to check on us. Our building was at the entrance of an underground railway tunnel and was always one of the main targets.

Gradually everything changed. At first, letters would still arrive, but then they came less frequently until they stopped altogether. Windows were blacked out, food and clothing coupons were introduced, and we had to go to the shelter night after night Most of the girls never saw their families again. I was one of the lucky ones – my parents and younger brother survived the war.

Courtesy of Susan Herold, Ra'anana, Israel

ERIC GOLDFARB

Eric (Eryk) was born in Chrzanów, Poland in December 1925. He had two older siblings: Hermann, born in 1919, and Sonja, born in 1920. Eric's family moved to Berlin, but he remained in Chrzanów with his aunt for the next two years before joining his family. Eric attended a Jewish school and joined a left-wing Zionist youth movement. In 1935 the family started looking for ways to emigrate together, but after Kristallnacht they felt they had to leave Germany even if it meant leaving separately.

In the early part of 1939 Erick's sister Sonja went to England with a *Habonim Hachshara* (Zionist Youth Movement). In 1941, she married an émigré from Vienna. In June 1939 Hermann left for Shanghai, where he later married.

In July 1939 Eric left Berlin on a Kindertransport to France. Eric was placed at the Quincy-sous-Senart chateau. Soon after the German occupation of France, Quincy had to be evacuated. Eric and some fifteen boys from a children's home were sent to a French boarding school in Clarmart. A few months later, in 1941, Eric moved to Chabannes, a large OSE children's home in Creuse, where he continued his formal schooling and learned leatherwork. For the next year and a half, Eric led a relatively trouble-free life, but this ended abruptly in August 1942, when the home was raided and some of the older children were arrested. Eric was sent to do agriculture work, the plan being that he would be able to flee from there to Spain and later join his mother in England. Eric was given a set of false papers and then told that instead of heading towards the Spanish border, he should go to Lyon to join other OSE youth who would be crossing the border to Switzerland. He and a group of five teenagers crossed the border but soon afterward, they ran into a Swiss guard who sent them back to France.

After many struggles, he and his friends joined the armed resistance in June 1944. Eric participated in heavy fighting and assisted in the liberation of Lyon. He remained with the Free French Forces until they reached the German border in October 1944. Not wanting to set foot again in Germany, Eric left the army and returned to Lyon. He stayed in Lyon from October 1944 to February 1945 and then went to Toulouse, where he found work as a bookbinder. He spent the summer working in a camp for Jewish orphans and then in the fall he moved to Paris, where he reconnected with many old friends, including Erica (his future wife).

During the spring of 1946, Eric went to England to see his mother and sister for the first time in seven years. He married in the summer of 1947. The couple moved to Paris where they had two children. Having accepted French citizenship in 1948, Eric was conscripted into the army. In July 1952, after his release from the army, the family immigrated to Canada to join Eric's sister and mother.

United States Holocaust Memorial Museum,
courtesy of Eric and Erica Goldfarb

TREVOR CHADWICK

(Kindertransport Rescuer)

Trevor Chadwick worked alongside Nicholas Winton. Trevor went to Prague in February 1939 and stayed there until mid-June 1939, playing a key role in organizing the Prague transports. He was given an office on Rubesova Street by a Czech cabinet minister which conveniently was located a block or so from Wilson Station. He had two assistants, who were thought to be volunteers. Trevor gathered information from parents who wanted their children out and then forwarded it to Nicholas Winton, who used every possible avenue in his search for foster homes. He played a major role in organizing the rail and ship transportations needed to get these children to England.

Many of the refugees who experienced these traumatic days full of strain and tension remember Trevor's wonderful disposition, his sense of humor, cheerfulness and sheer determination. It is thought that Trevor left Prague in June 1939 directly after seeing off 123 children on board a Kindertransport. Even in his absence, the system that he played such a major role in putting into place continued with great efficiency and resolve.

Courtesy of Charles Chadwick, England
For more information see: The Rescue of the Prague Refugees 1938/39
by William R. Chadwick

ALFRED SCHWARZKOPF

Alfred, a Jewish refugee boy from the Kindertransport, at Rowden Hall School in Margate, England, where he was a member of the school's soccer team.

United States Holocaust Memorial Museum,
courtesy of Guenther Cahn

R obert was born in August 1928 in Liberec (Reichenberg), Czechoslovakia. He lived in Liberec until August/September 1938, when, as a result of the 'Munich Agreement' signed in September 1938, he moved to Prague.

In March 1939 Germany had absorbed the remainder of Czechoslovakia. On the advice of a friend living in London who worked on behalf of the refugees, Robert was made ready with just 24-hours' notice to leave on a Kindertransport organized by Nicholas Winton, which left Prague at the end of June 1939.

Robert's mother and sister eventually left Prague via Genoa on an Italian boat, before Italy entered the war. They arrived in New Zealand in May 1940. Robert left England for New Zealand in August 1940, and arrived in Auckland in October 1940. Within a few days he was fully employed and remained so until his retirement. In January 1943 Robert volunteered for the New Zealand Air Force and was called up in June 1943. One year later he was awarded his wings and was commissioned as a Pilot Officer and later a Flying Officer. In January 1946 he was discharged, and a few months later he started his architectural training. Robert worked as an architect until 2000.

Liberec, Czech Republic

Courtesy of Robert Fantl, Wilton, Wellington, New Zealand

Train Thirty

Ilse was born in August 1925 in Krems on the Danube, Lower Austria. She left Austria on the second Kindertransport on December 18, 1938. She arrived at Harwich, from where the *kinder* were sent to Dovercourt camp. A few days later, the Quakers came and took her to live with a gentile family in Welwyn Garden City (north of London).

Ilse's sister Herta Gilbert (née Blau) left on the first Kindertransport and lives in Melbourne, Australia.

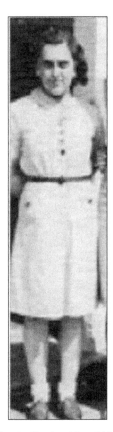

Ilse in England in 1939 having just completed her last year of schooling, a total of seven months since arriving from Austria.

Ilse (left) with her sister Herta Gilbert (née Blau) in Austria in 1938.

Courtesy of Carol Shotts, Zichron Yaacov, Israel

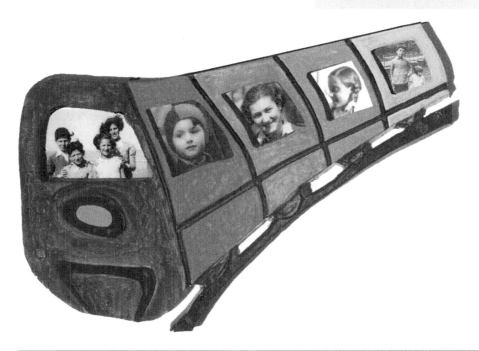

MARION HOUSE (NÉE SAUERBRUNN)

Marion was born in February 1923 in Berlin. She attended a private school in Berlin until she and other Jewish students were told it would be 'best' if they found a new school. Marion's life became more pleasant in the new school, as she was surrounded by other Jewish children. After Kristallnacht, Marion's parents thought hard about emigrating but decided to remain in Germany because they did not want to abandon her 82-year-old grandfather. However, they were anxious for Marion's safety and managed to get her a place on a Kindertransport. In May 1939 Marion left Berlin and, at sixteen, she was one of the oldest children on the transport. After the war she was reunited with her parents in Deggendorf displaced persons camp in Germany. They had survived the Theresienstadt concentration camp. The family immigrated to the United States and settled in New York.

United States Holocaust Memorial Museum, courtesy of Marion House

JACOB ZAJAC

JOSEPH ZAJAC

ANNI (ANNA) ZAJAC

HENNI ZAJAC

Anni (see page 179), Henni, Jacob and Joseph remained in the *Beith Ahawah Kinderheim* ('House of Love' children's home) on Auguststrasse in Berlin, until December 1938, when they went on the second Kindertransport to England. The children spent one night in Dovercourt in Harwich and then were sent to an Orthodox hostel in Willesden, in northwest London. One month later, Jacob celebrated his Bar Mitzvah. He was the first Kindertransport boy to celebrate his Bar Mitzvah in England.

Beith Ahawah was paid for by the Jewish Council and housed approximately 120 Jewish children from Eastern Europe. With such serious the economic problems, many parents could not support their children and asked for the school to care for them.

Railroad Station,
Manheim, Germany

United States Holocaust Memorial Museum, courtesy of Anna Leist

PETER NEEDHAM

Peter was a very young boy when he left Prague with other children on a Kindertransport flight organized by the Barbican Mission in 1939.

Barbican Mission

Courtesy of the Imperial War Museum, London, UK

OLGA (LEVY) DRUCKER (NÉE LENK)

Olga was born in Stuttgart, Germany on December 28, 1927. She left Stuttgart on a Kindertransport arriving at Harwich on March 3, 1939, from the Hook of Holland. She went to London, where she was met by her brother. Olga was only eleven years old. Her parents eventually were able to leave Germany and make their way to New York. Olga spent six years in England before she was reunited with them there in March 1945. She met her husband Rolf, a Holocaust survivor from Berlin, in New York. She has three children and two grandchildren.

Courtesy of Kindertransport by Olga Drucker, Palm City, Florida, USA

ZEEV BERKLEY (FORMERLY WOLFGANG BACKHAUS)

GABY ZAHAVI (NÉE GABRIELLA BACKHAUS)

Wolfgang was born in December 1925 in Eisenach (Thueringen), Germany. His sister Gabriella was born in April 1929, also in Eisenach. They came from a very well respected family. Their father, Dr. Alfred Backhaus, was a lawyer (public prosecutor). In 1936, as a Jew, he could no longer practice as a lawyer. He took a revolver and he killed himself in his office located in the town hall. Their mother, Chana Backhaus, a very beautiful woman, was left a young widow. She took both Wolfgang and Gabriella and moved to Berlin to live with her mother. In 1939 both Wolfgang and Gabriella were sent to safety to England on a Kindertransport.

Although he was only thirteen years old, Wolfgang felt very responsible for his little sister. Gabriella was taken to live with a Jewish family who had no children and wanted to adopt her. Wolfgang was also taken in by a Jewish family, but when they were evacuated from London, they could not take him with them. He then had some very hard years moving from farm to farm, with no family. At the age of seventeen he joined a kibbutz *Hachshara* and life began to take a better turn. He joined the British Army and later served in the Jewish Brigade.

Meanwhile, Wolfgang's mother Chana managed to reach Palestine. She remarried and was able to organize Gabriella's safe passage to join her. Gabriella joined the *Palmach*[8] and met her husband there. They lived on a kibbutz and had four children. Wolfgang married Ruth and had two children. Both siblings remained very close all their lives.

Photo and text courtesy of Ruth Berkley, Israel

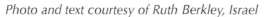

8. The elite striking force of the *Haganah*, the underground military organization of the Jews in Palestine prior to the establishment of the State of Israel.

GROUP OF *KINDER* WAVING GOODBYE

A group of *kinder* leaving Prague on a Kindertransport to England in 1939.

Courtesy of the Imperial War Museum, London, UK

Train 32

157

DORRITH SIM (NÉE OPPENHEIM)

Dorrith was born in August 1931 in Kassel, Germany. She was seven and a half years of age when she left Hamburg on a Kindertransport in July 1939 en route to Holland, arriving in England on July 26, 1939. From there, she traveled to Edinburgh, Scotland, arriving on July 28, 1939.

Courtesy of Dorrith M. Sim, Prestwick, Ayrshire, Scotland, UK

EDITH ROTHSCHILD

Edith was born in May 1925 in Frankfurt. In May 1939 she left Frankfurt on a Kindertransport to England. She arrived at Liverpool Street Station in London the following day and continued her journey to Cambridge.

Edith Rothschild ID papers

Courtesy of Edith Rothschild, UK

TRUDE ROSA ROTHSCHILD

Trude left Frankfurt at the end of March 1939. She arrived at Liverpool Street Station the following day. That same day she continued her journey to Cambridge.

Courtesy of Edith Rothschild, UK

RUTH MORLEY (NÉE BIRNHOLZ)

Ruth was born in Vienna in November 1925. She left Vienna in January 1939 and arrived in London where a family friend, herself a refugee from Vienna, met her at the station and took her to the first of many foster homes. Eventually, Ruth was placed with a family who had a girl her age and a younger brother. Ruth stayed with them for over a year until she was able to be reunited with her parents, who had arrived in the UK before the start of the war, but because they were refugees without a home, they had been unable to take her to live with them. Ruth and her parents sailed to New York in August 1940. She was very close to her foster family and that closeness remained all her life. Her daughter, Melissa, stays in contact with Ruth's foster siblings when she travels to Edinburgh or to Toronto.

Ruth became an award-winning costume designer for film and theater.

Photo and text courtesy of Melissa Hacker (daughter of Ruth Morley),
director of the film My Knees Were Jumping: Remembering the Kindertransports

LIESL SILVERSTONE (NÉE FISCHMANNOVA)

Liesl was born in Teplice-Sanov, Czechoslovakia, in June 1927. In July 1939 Liesl arrived at Liverpool Street Station from Prague with Nicholas Winton's Kindertransport.

Courtesy of Liesl Silverstone, London, UK

JOHN FIELDSEND (FORMERLY HANS HEINI FEIGE)

John was born in Czechoslovakia. In July 1939 he arrived in England on one of the Kindertransports organized by Nicholas Winton.

Courtesy of John Fieldsend, UK

OTTO DEUTSCH

Otto was born in Vienna in July 1928. His sister, Adele, was born in June 1921. Otto left Vienna on a Kindertransport to England in July 1939, just one week before his eleventh birthday. Sadly, his sister was too old to qualify for the Kindertransport. Otto was given shelter in the loving home of a Christian family in the northeast of England.

Sadly, his dear parents and sister perished in the death camp of Maly Trostinec, which is about sixteen miles from Minsk, the capital of Belarus.

Courtesy of Otto Deutsch, Southend-on-Sea, UK

A young Jewish girl in search of a safe haven, wearing a tag with the number 247, sits on a suitcase, her head in her hands, after arriving in England with the second Kindertransport.

United States Holocaust Memorial Museum, courtesy of National Archives and Records Administration, College Park

ALFRED TRAUM

Alfred was born in March 1929 in Vienna, where his parents ran a business. Alfred had an older sister, Ruth, who was born in March 1926. Alfred attended a public school, but in March 1938, when Germany annexed Austria, life changed dramatically. Ruth and Alfred were forced out of their school and went to a Jewish school farther away from home. After Kristallnacht, his parents heard about a Kindertransport and the opportunity for him to be sent with his sister to England. His parents hoped they would be able to obtain visas and join them, but sadly this never happened. A business colleague of Alfred's father arranged for Alfred and Ruth to be placed with a family in England and in June 1939, they left Vienna on a Kindertransport. Their parents were not so fortunate. After the war ended, Alfred learned that they had perished.

The Kiddush Cup
by Alfred Traum

It was always the same. Ushering the Sabbath, my father held the silver *Kiddush* cup in the flat palm of his hand with his thumb resting against the brim of the cup, his head held high, eyes half closed as he recited the blessing over the wine. We all took a sip from the Kiddush cup. That and all the other festive traditional activities were carried out in their proper order. Any bystander would have thought this was just an ordinary Friday night in a Jewish home. So it would have seemed. But I am sure that both our parents' hearts were breaking. My sister and I were leaving for England on the following Wednesday. This would be our last Sabbath dinner together. Although we thought that we would soon be reunited, our parents knew the difficulties that lay ahead. And indeed it was the last Sabbath meal we shared.

Preparing for the Sabbath actually began Thursdays, with my mother laying out large, round, thinly rolled dough that would later be used to make noodles for soup. She busied herself in the kitchen all evening making a mouth-watering selection of cakes that would last through the week. We never bought any ready-made cakes. Everything was home made. That particular week she would need more since many friends and relatives would drop in, say their goodbyes and wish us well on our journey. Friday morning I would watch, as I had watched so many times in the past, as she plaited the dough to make the *challot*, then baste them with egg yolks and lightly sprinkle poppy seeds on them before placing them in the oven. The aromas from the baking and food preparation were a symphony to the nose. A rare and wonderful smell that, even now, can whisk me back in time when on a rare occasion, something comes close to it. This was the routine in our home, and very likely in many other Jewish homes in Vienna.

My father was crippled as a result of his service in the Austrian

Army in World War I. I never really knew what his exact diagnosis was, but he could only get around with the aid of two canes. He never complained about his handicap and was always cheerful and a pleasure to be around. However, when he was seated, there was nothing that he could not do. He had gifted hands that could turn to so many things. Fabulous at drawing, he taught me so much: how to use proportions, to take perspectives into account when creating a drawing. Although never trained to be a tailor, he handled the sewing machine like a professional, making all kinds of clothes for us, even a new suit for me. He could turn his hands to all sorts of activities: resole shoes, repair electric apparatus, even tinker with the radio when it went on the blink and somehow he got it functioning again. He was an amateur photographer and did his own developing and printing. We never went to a photography studio and, as a result, we only have little snap shots, which he had done himself. I used to watch him closely, picking up many cues, which I would store away for use for some future day. I learned so much from him, but most of all he taught me how to live with adversities and make the most of everything.

Sometimes, when I was rebuilding an engine for the car, or building an addition to our home, some of my friends would ask me, 'Where did you learn how to do that?' I would simply shrug my shoulders, but in the back of my mind was my father telling me, 'Go ahead, you can do it.' Perhaps it sounds far-fetched, but he taught me so much without leaving his chair.

On the Wednesday of our departure we all went downstairs to the backyard where my father set up the tripod and camera, placed a black cloth over his head and had us all assemble for him to take a picture. He selected the delayed shutter, so he could join us for the picture to be taken. A short while later, it was time for us depart for the West Bahnhof, the railroad station for trains heading west. As we were about to leave, my dad said to me, '*Go forward, don't look back, just go forward.*' I was never quite sure what he meant, but believe it to have been more philosophical than in the literal manner a small child would take it. However, as the three of us proceeded along the sidewalk, and we were still only a short distance from our home, I did stop to turn around to look back, and just as I expected, my father was at the bay window with tears in his eyes, attempting to force a smile, while watching my sister and I walk out of his life.

When the photograph had been developed, a copy was sent to us in England. It captured all of our feelings. It is the saddest picture I have ever seen; nevertheless, it is a treasured memento of that day. On one of the negatives my father had written (in German) '*die abshied*' – the farewell'.

At the train station, the platform was crowded with parents coming to see their children off on the Kindertransport and to a new life in England, hoping they would not forget their old lives and those who loved them. It was a train specially scheduled just for our group, probably a couple of hundred kids, from real little ones scarcely more than toddlers, up to the age of seventeen. My sister and I stood at an open window holding hands with our mother. She too was fighting back tears, trying to tell us that it would be just for a short while. In retrospect, I don't think she believed her own words, but what else could she

Alfred's passport

say? We were bravely looking at each other not knowing what to say when suddenly my classroom teacher, Professor Schwartzbard, appeared in front of us. He knew I was leaving on the Kindertransport on that day and apparently had managed to have his young son accepted too. He was holding his five-year-old son like a piece of luggage under his arm. The professor passed his son through the open window, asking if he could sit with us and that I might keep an eye out for him until we reached London, where someone would come to pick him up. Naturally I agreed. Instantly I felt all grown up with newfound responsibilities dropped in my lap.

A whistle blew and we kissed and hugged through the open window and reluctantly let go of each other as the train began to pull away. My mother tried running along with the train holding on to our hands but not for long. Soon her lonely figure diminished as we snaked our way out of the station. She had just passed the hardest test that could befall any parent.

All our belongings were in our two large rucksacks, stuffed to the brim with clothing plus lots of sweets and chocolates that friends and relatives had given us. My parents sent along a very nice box of chocolates for the Griggs family who had agreed to take us into their home. We were not permitted to bring along any valuables, jewelry or money. If found it would be confiscated or bring us even more trouble. I hid the watch my parents had given me for my tenth birthday and didn't remove it from its hiding place until we reached Holland.

This writing is not about our time in England, but rather about two dates: June 20, 1939, our departure from Vienna, and June 24, 1958, the day of our wedding.

My sister had come from Israel to be with us at our wedding. She had a very special gift for me. One that she had been saving for such an occasion. It was my father's Kiddush cup. The same cup I had seen on so many Friday nights. My father had taken an enormous risk and stuffed the cup amongst my sister's clothing, not telling her in order not to frighten her, but knowing that she was mature enough and would know what to do with it and when the moment was right to pass it on to me. And my wedding day was that moment. But more importantly, in parting with his Kiddush cup, which he probably received on some special occasion, he must have been acutely aware of severity of their situation and the doubtfulness of their survival. It is my most prized possession. Every Friday evening, as we usher in the Sabbath, it graces our table. Perhaps I don't hold it in the same manner as he did, but I recite the same blessing over the wine and I look around at my family and count my blessings, and I think: *'How fortunate I am to have had such parents.'*

Alfred Traum

Text courtesy of Alfred Traum, Washington, D.C., USA

Train 34

ARTUR SPIRO

MAX SPIRO

Artur and Max from Hamm, Germany, are pictured at the Priory, a children's home in Selkirk, Scotland.

United States Holocaust Memorial Museum, courtesy of Gunther Abrahamson

EDITH LUNZER

Edith was born in December 1922 in Vienna. In April 1939 she left Vienna on a Kindertransport and came to London via the Port of Harwich.

Photo thought to be Edith Lunzer, courtesy of The Wiener Library for the Study of the Holocaust & Genocide, London, UK

EVA ABRAHAM-PODIETZ (NÉE ROSENBAUM)

HEINZ ROSENBAUM

Eva was born in May 1927 in Hamburg, Germany. Her brother Heinz was born in 1924. During the summer of 1938, Eva and Heinz's father moved to England and made preparations for his family to join him. Heinz followed him in September after being sponsored by a British woman who provided sponsorship to a number of German Jewish refugee children.

In December 1938 Eva left for England on the second Kindertransport. After arriving at Harwich, she was taken to a temporary shelter at the nearby Dovercourt Bay holiday camp. A few weeks later, Eva was sent to live with a foster family in Nottingham, where she worked as a nanny for their two-year-old daughter. Neither Eva nor her brother, who was living with another family in Nottingham, was able to join their father. He did not have the means to house and support them. Eva's mother was the last to reach England, arriving in August 1939.

After her parents found an apartment in London, Eva moved in with them. A few weeks later she and her classmates were evacuated to Northampton, where she stayed with a series of foster families over the next three years. In the fall of 1942 Eva returned to London, where she matriculated and received training as a teacher and social worker. After the war Eva worked for the American Jewish Joint Distribution Committee assisting Jewish displaced persons in Germany and Brazil.

Hamburg, Germany

United States Holocaust Memorial Museum, courtesy of Eva Rosenbaum Abraham-Podietz

Vera was born in Prague in January 1930. At the end of May 1939, she left Prague on a Kindertransport and arrived at Liverpool Street Station in London two days later, in June 1939.

Vera's passport

Vera at the Hook of Holland with a relative and a friend of her parents, taken May 30, 1939.

Courtesy of Vera Schaufeld, London, UK

MARTIN EISEMAN

Martin was a young Jewish refugee in Nottingham, where he lived after he arrived in England on a Kindertransport in 1939.

Courtesy of the United States Holocaust Memorial Museum

MAX SCHWARTZ

SZYMON KLITENIK

JUNI SCHWARTZ

JACK SCHWARTZ

MAX SCHEINFELD

MAX SCHWARTZ

SZYMON KLITENIK

JUNI SCHWARTZ

JACK SCHWARTZ

MAX SCHEINFELD

Max, Szymon, Juni, Jack and Max (Scheinfeld) arrived in England on a Kindertransport. They later boarded the *SS Oronsay* en route to Australia.

United States Holocaust Memorial Museum, courtesy of Dr. Glen Palmer

Train 36

GROUP OF KINDER

Jewish refugee children: Werner Rindsberg, Rosalie Johnson (née Blau), Toni Rosenblatt, Ruth Rosenblatt, Regina Rosenblatt, Lotte Nussbaum, Inge Joseph and Edith Rosenthal (née Goldapper) outside the children's home in Zuen, Belgium.

United States Holocaust Memorial Museum, courtesy of Walter Reed

GERHARD ROSENZWEIG

Gerhard was a Jewish refugee boy who was sent to France on a Kindertransport in the spring of 1939. He stayed at a chateau at Quincy-sous-Senart, which was located close to Paris. Quincy served as a Jewish children's home until September 1940 when, following the German occupation of France, the German army took control of it. The boys were then relocated to other OSE homes.

United States Holocaust Memorial Museum, courtesy of Stephan H. Lewy

STEPHEN KOLLISCH

Stephen, Peter and Eva Kollisch (see page 70) were sent by their parents on a Kindertransport from Vienna to England in July 1939. They stayed with a Quaker family in Bristol for about six months before receiving their immigration papers for the United States. On their arrival in the United States in March 1940, the Kollisch siblings were reunited with their parents, who had fled Vienna in the fall of 1939.

Vienna center

United States Holocaust Memorial Museum, courtesy of Peter Kollisch

Paul was born in Baden-bei-Wien, Austria, in November 1930. At the time of the *Anschluss* in March 1938, when Nazi Germany occupied Austria, he and his parents reached Bratislava.

In 1939 he was one of ten boys to have a place on a Kindertransport train organized by Sir Nicholas Winton. Paul reached England in June 1939. When World War II broke out, Paul was evacuated to Chatteris in Cambridgeshire, where he spent the war years in the care of a Baptist minister. In 1945 he returned to

Paul with his parents

London to continue his education at the Davenant Foundation School in Whitechapel. Meanwhile, his parents escaped from Europe and set up home in Haifa, Israel, where Paul joined them in 1949 after a ten-year separation.

Paul served in the Israel Defense Forces until 1954. Upon his release he joined the *Jerusalem Post* as a reporter in Tel Aviv and a feature writer. Later he became the paper's military correspondent and Tel Aviv stringer for the Associated Press. He was also a correspondent for the *London Jewish Observer*. For the Associated Press, he reported on the Six-Day War in 1967 and Yom Kippur War in 1973, and co-authored the Associated Press's book on the Six-Day War entitled *Lightning Out of Israel*.

In 1969 Paul started a three-year stint as a Jewish Agency emissary in London dealing with *aliyah* (immigration to Israel). After returning to Israel, he lived in Herzliya, where he went into the real estate business while continuing as a sports writer with the *Jerusalem Post*.

Paul married Hannah Moschytz in Zurich in 1960. She has since sadly passed away. They had two sons and two daughters, all of whom are married and live in Israel, and between them have eleven children.

Courtesy of Paul Kohn, Herzliya, Israel

Train 37

ANNELIESE FISCHER

Anneliese was born in 1925 in Berlin. She left on a Kindertransport to Hamburg, Germany in December 1938. In Hamburg, Anneliese surrendered her passport and boarded an American liner, the *SS Washington*, and sailed to Le Havre, France, and from there to Southampton, England, where she arrived on December 30, 1928. From Southampton, she took a train to her final destination, Waterloo Station, where her new foster family picked her up. She was identified by a large sign hanging around her neck with the name and address of the family taking her in.

Courtesy of Anne F. Heineman (née Anneliese Fischer), author of My Nine Lives, *Irvine, California, USA*

Joseph was born in Fulda, Germany, on March 9, 1924. He was the only child of Fredrick and Gerda Braunold. Joseph left Fulda on a Kindertransport that left Frankfurt for England on July 26, 1939, arriving at Harwich (via the Hook of Holland) and then on to Liverpool Street Station in London. Upon arrival in London, Joseph was sent to the Jewish Refugee Hostel in Cardiff, Wales. Fredrick and Gerda Braunold were both deported to concentrations camps: Fredrick to the Jungfernhof camp in Latvia in 1942 when he was fifty-four, and Gerda to the Stutthof camp in Danzig in 1944 when she was fifty-one. They both perished.

On June 27, 1940, at the age of sixteen, Joseph was arrested in Cardiff by the British authorities for being an alien in the UK and was interned in the Isle of Man with other German Jews who had managed to leave Germany before the outbreak of war. Joseph was released a year later and went back to London, where he spent the war years working at various jobs trying to earn basic funds and, where possible, to help in the war effort. After the war, he met his future wife Ruth at the Jewish Refugee Hostel located in Willesden Lane, London.

Ruth Beer was born in Leipzig on January 28, 1927. She was the only child of Lea and Gershon Beer. Ruth left on a Kindertransport departing from Leipzig and arrived in London on July 14, 1939. On  arrival at Liverpool Street Station she was taken to a girls' hostel in Kingstonley, Gloucestershire. Ruth and Joseph arrived three weeks apart on Kindertransport trains, both via the Hook of Holland. Ruth's father Gershon was arrested for being of Polish Jewish origin immediately after Kristallnacht in November 1938 and deported from Leipzig to the Polish border. He was never located thereafter. At the time, he was sixty-one. Ruth's mother Lea was deported to Riga on January 21, 1942, and German records indicate that she was murdered upon arrival. She was fifty-one years old.

Joseph and Ruth as refugees met socially via Jewish groups in London and were married in May 1948. Joseph was twenty-four and Ruth was twenty-one. In 1949 they moved to Glasgow in Scotland and then to Sunderland in northern England, where they both became prominent members of the local Jewish community. They had three sons, and eight grandchildren. Joseph and Ruth spent the rest of their lives in England.

Courtesy of Michael Braunold (son), Raanana, Israel

Train 38

WALTER HERZIG

Walter was a German Jewish refugee who was sent to France on a Kindertransport in the spring of 1939, to the children's home Quincy-sous-Senart, near Paris.

United States Holocaust Memorial Museum,
courtesy of Stephan H. Lewy

ROSALIE JOHNSON (NÉE BLAU)

Rosalie was a Jewish refugee in the children's home in Zuen, Brussels.

United States Holocaust Memorial Museum,
courtesy of Walter Reed

MARGOT HIRSCH

Margot was born in Frankfurt. She left Germany for England on a Kindertransport in 1939, when she was fourteen years old.

Courtesy of Alisa Tennenbaum, Bet Cherut, Israel

Suse was born in May 6, 1931, in Worms, Germany. Her parents were Flora (née Hirsch) and Albert Herz. Her sister is Edith Herz Lucas Pagelson. In July 1938, aged eight, Suse left from the train station in Mainz, Germany, on a Kindertransport to England.

Suse (left) and Edith Herz in Germany

When she arrived at Harwich she was met by Mr. Laxon and Mr. Overton and taken to Kenilworth, along with three other young refugees.

Suse lived in Coventry, England, with foster parents Florrie and George Parry and foster brothers David and John. During a period of intense bombing, she was evacuated to Cuddington, a village in Cheshire in northern England, and stayed with Leslie and Sibyl Evans. After a time she returned back to the Parrys, but in 1944 she went to a hostel located in Wheeleys Road in Birmingham. In May 1946 Suse arrived in New York and nine months later, in February 1947, at Pier 84 in New York City, she was reunited with her mother and sister who had survived Auschwitz.

Suse married Walter Rosenstock in 1950 and they lived in Monmouth Junction, New Jersey and San Diego, California. They had three children, Elaine, Alan and Deborah. They had four grandchildren, Ross and Larissa Peizer and Max and Sam Rosenstock. Suse passed away in April 2002. She was predeceased by her son, Alan. Suse's mother lived to the age of 84. Her sister Edith currently resides in Maine, USA.

*Courtesy of Deborah Rosenstock, Edgewater, New Jersey
and Elaine Peizer, Seattle, Washington, USA*

Anni was born in January 1925 in Manheim, Germany, where her father worked as a self-employed tailor. Her parents, Wolf and Dora, came from Zgierz, near Lodz in Poland. After they married, they moved to Manheim where their children Felix, Samuel, Anni, Jacob (Jack), Henni, Joseph and Lydia were born. In 1930 they moved to Berlin, where Dora gave birth to twins, Hella and Hermann. The Zajacs had two additional children, who sadly died in infancy.

In 1935 Wolf was deported to Posnan, Poland. The rest of the family should have gone as well except that Dora was suffering from tuberculosis and was too unwell to follow him. A year later, in 1936, her health further deteriorated, so she placed the seven younger children in the *Beith Ahawah* children's home. The two older brothers, Felix and Samuel, stayed with their mother until she passed away in January 1938. About four months after she died, Samuel left Germany to join his father in Poland and Felix joined the *Hachshara* in Berlin only to be deported to Poland in October 1938. The two brothers joined a new *Hachshara* in Warsaw and, after the start of World War II, escaped to Vilna. They reached Palestine eight months later, lived on a kibbutz and eventually joined the Jewish Brigade.

Anni, Henni, Jacob and Joseph remained at *Beith Ahawah* until December 1938, when they were sent on the second Kindertransport to England. They spent one night in Dovercourt at Harwich and then were sent to an Orthodox hostel in Willesden in northwest London. Lydia, Hella and Hermann remained in Berlin, but after their mother's death they were transferred to different children's homes.

Lydia came to England on a Kindertransport in August 1939 and was placed in various foster homes. The twins, Hella and Hermann, were sent to Sweden and spent the war there. At the start of the war, the other children became separated. Jack and Joseph were sent to live in Margate for a short time and then returned to London. Henni and Anni were evacuated to the country. Henni remained there while Anni returned to London and worked in an ammunition factory. Twice she was bombed out and had to move to a new hostel. Henni and Joseph eventually joined her. Jacob joined the Jewish Brigade and unexpectedly met up with Felix and Samuel in Naples, Italy.

Though their father perished in the Holocaust having been incarcerated in the Lublin ghetto, all nine children survived. After the war Jacob, Anni, Joseph, Henni and Lydia immigrated to the United States. Hella remained in Sweden. Hermann immigrated to Israel to join his older brothers Samuel and Felix.

Manheim Castle, Germany

United States Holocaust Memorial Museum, courtesy of Anna Leist

HERBERT ROSENTHAL

Herbert was born in February 1924 in Frankfurt. His younger brother Manfred was born in September 1926. In February 1939, just before Herbert turned fifteen, he was sent on a Kindertransport to England. While there, he studied at a technical school in Kent. When Herbert turned sixteen, however, he was considered an enemy alien and deported to Australia. In July 1940 Herbert found himself on the *HMT Dunera* set for Sydney, Australia. His parents, in the meantime, found a safe haven in the United States. They had been able to escape via Lisbon to New York. However, Manfred was in France and lived throughout the war under the protection of the OSE at Chateau de Chaumont, Mainsat, Creuse and Chateau Montintin.

Frankfurt, Germany

United States Holocaust Memorial Museum, courtesy of Manfred Rosenthal

Train 39

REFUGEE CHILDREN CELEBRATE CHANUKAH

A group of young Jewish refugee children gathered together from the Rowden Hall School in Margate, England, attend a Chanukah party in an overflow hostel.

United States Holocaust Memorial Museum, courtesy of Guenther Cahn

RUTH CALMON MOOS

I n 1936 Ruth left Germany by train from Berlin to Hamburg, where she boarded a ship with a group of '1,000 Children' for the United States. She was thirteen years old.

Courtesy of Ruth Moos, Laguna Hills, California, USA

YOUNG JEWISH REFUGEE CHILDREN

Members of the Rowden Hall School soccer team, Margate, England

Rowden Hall School

United States Holocaust Memorial Museum, courtesy of Guenther Cahn

SONJA KLEINER

HANA KLEINER

Sonja was aged thirteen and Hana was twelve when they boarded a Kindertransport from Hradec Králové, Czechoslovakia to England. They arrived in early August 1939 on the last train from Prague.

Courtesy of Hana Kleiner, London, UK

EVA BRUMMELOVA

Eva was born in July 1923 and her younger sister Lilly was born in March 1926. In July 1939 Eva left for England on one of Nicholas Winton's Kindertransports. Lilly did not want to go away and her mother was grateful that at least one of her daughters would stay.

When Eva came to England she was fifteen years old and alone. She spoke Czech, German and French, but very little English.

After a short period with an English family, where she had no opportunity to study, she contacted friends of her parents in Birmingham who took her in and funded her studies for one year. She became a dispensing chemist and worked at a doctor's surgery through the war years. At the end of the war she moved to Bristol, where she was a medical researcher.

In 1955 Eva married Michael Brian Nelson from Bristol. Their daughter Susan was born in June 1958 and she also lives in Bristol. Gillian was born in November 1959 and she settled down in Worthing in West Sussex. Eva has four grandchildren. Lilly and the rest of Eva's family did not survive.

Courtesy of Sue Taylor, Bristol, UK

Train 40

MARIETTA DRUCKER (NÉE SOBEL)

Marietta was born in Vienna on July 3, 1928. In January 1939 she left on a Kindertransport to England. She lived in various foster homes. Her parents, Peppie and Poldi, eventually managed to escape and arrived in England a few months later. Marietta was able to see them, but only briefly and on rare occasions. After the war, about seven years later, she was finally reunited with them. In 1951 she left London for New York, while her parents remained in England. She met her husband shortly after her arrival and within just a few weeks they were engaged. A year later, in 1952, they married. Marietta has two daughters and five grandsons.

Courtesy of Marietta Drucker, St. Petersburg, Florida, USA

ISOLDE LILLI NETTER

Isolde (Lilli) was born in November 1923 in Goppingen. Lilli left on a Kindertransport to England in February 1939.

Courtesy of Ellen Silk, Sherman Oaks, California, USA

BEA GREEN (NÉE MARIA BEATE SIEGEL)

Bea was born in March 1925 in Munich, Germany. She is the daughter of Michael and Mathilde (née Waldner) Siegel. Her father was a prominent lawyer and her mother was an artist. Bea remembers vividly that day in March 1933 when her father, one of the first victims of terror and one of the few to survive it, was beaten up, and then forced to parade barefooted with a sign saying: 'I am a Jew and will never again complain to the police.'

Just before midnight on June 27, 1939, fourteen-year-old Bea left on a Kindertransport to England. She went to live in a very English setting with a retired colonel and his aristocratic wife – learning how to dry-fly fish on the River Itchen (in Hampshire in southern England) and how to train gun dogs! It certainly taught her a great deal about English life. In 1942 the family enrolled her into university and she became an academic and later was appointed a magistrate[9].

Bea fulfilled her childhood desire to become a lawyer, a mother and an opera singer. She has three sons, sings in a choir and retired from the bench (law court) in the mid-1990s.

Courtesy of Bea Green, London, UK

---

9. Magistrates are trained, unpaid members of their local community, who work part-time and deal with less serious criminal cases.

LUCIE LAQUER

Lucie, a young German refugee, became the matron at the Whittingehame *Hachshara*. The young people flourished under her great care. Among those who took an active interest in the Whittingehame shelter was Vera Weizmann, the wife of Chaim Weizmann, who later became the first President of Israel.

Courtesy of the United States Holocaust Memorial Museum

HANNAH KRAG

Hannah left Munich, Germany, on a Kindertransport and arrived in England in April 1939. Hannah was interned at the Rushen Camp for a few months on the Isle of Man, which was used as a center for holding enemy aliens during both World Wars. In 1946 Hannah came to the United States.

Courtesy of the United States Holocaust Memorial Museum

EDITH MOSER

Edith was a German Jewish refugee child who stayed in an orphanage in Belgium, where she and a group of other children were sent on a Kindertransport.

Courtesy of the United States Holocaust Memorial Museum, courtesy of Hans and Ilse Garfunkel

Train 41

GERALD LEYENS

Gerald was born in Erkelez, Germany. He was thirteen when he arrived in England on a Kindertransport.

Courtesy of Gerald Leyens, London, UK

EDITH MESCH-REISFELD

Edith was born in Wiesbaden, Germany. After Kristallnacht in November 1938, Edith and her parents fled from their home and business to Aachen, a German town that bordered on Belgium. After much unrest, they managed to get themselves into Belgium. Edith's parents knew the war was imminent and their prime concern was her safety. Edith was eleven years old in August 1939 when her parents put her on a Kindertransport bound for the boat sailing to England. She had many difficult and lonely times in England. Her parents were able to survive and after seven years of separation from them, they were finally reunited together as a family.

Courtesy of Edith Mesch-Reisfeld, New Hyde Park, New York, USA

MARGOT GOLDBERG

Margot was born in Düsseldorf, Germany in February 1926. In June 1939 she left on a Kindertransport to England. She was thirteen years old.

Düsseldorf, Germany

Courtesy of Margot Goldberg, Palo Alto, California, USA

JOE HESS

Joe was born in Fulda, Germany, in June 1932. He was only six years old and his sister Ilsa was twelve when they left on a Kindertransport to England in March 1939.

Courtesy of Joe Hess, Orange County, California, USA

BERND KOSCHLAND

Bernd was born in January 1931 in Fuerth, Bavaria, near Nuremberg in Germany. He arrived in England on a Kindertransport at the end of March 1939 and went to a hostel in Margate (Kent), a town on the coast of southeast England.

Courtesy of Bernd Koschland, London, UK

Ruth was born in Cloppenburg, Germany, about 150 miles northwest of the Dutch border. Her sister Hilde was fifteen months younger. In 1936 it was no longer permitted for Jewish students to attend local schools. The nearest Jewish school was about a two-hour commute. After Kristallnacht their family house was plastered with swastikas. Her sisters were in tears, as was their mother, and their father was taken away. The following day Ruth and Hilde's mother received word that their father 'might' have been left behind in a hospital and Ruth was sent to check all the hospitals in the area, but to no avail. Shortly after this, Ruth's mother was given permission to send two of her children to England on a Kindertransport. Ruth and Hilde, the two middle girls, were the ones to leave in early December 1938. Later that same month their father was released.

Meanwhile in England, Ruth and Hilde had a rough crossing but finally arrived at Harwich. Many Jewish and non-Jewish families came forward to offer their homes, but Ruth and Hilde decided to go with a Jewish group of congregants that offered care to twenty-five girls in a hostel in Harrogate, Yorkshire, for religious girls.

In May 1939 Ruth and Hilde's parents boarded the fateful *St. Louis* to Cuba. After sailing around the Caribbean and South Florida the ship was turned away and sent back to Europe. England, Belgium, France and Holland offered refuge to more than 900 passengers. Their parents went to Holland.

When Hitler invaded Holland, they were sent to the Westerbork transit camp, and in May 1943 they were sent to the Sobibor concentration camp, where they perished. This Ruth only learned after the war. In the meantime, Edith, the third and oldest sister, had left Holland for America. Ruth and Hilde arrived in the USA in January 1945.

Courtesy of Ruth Heinemann, Lantana, Florida, USA

Ossi was born in Leipzig, Germany. In July 1939, at the age of fifteen, he left on a Kindertransport from Leipzig, arriving at Harwich the following day. He and some children were taken to London and from there they were separated into three groups. The children under the age of ten were sent to live with families; those aged between ten and fifteen were put into hostels. Ossi spent a short time in London and then in various hostels in Wales, Manchester and London.

Kindertransport survivor Oskar, aged 22, in the British Army in 1945

After a couple of years, Ossi joined the British Army, eventually working as an interpreter in Hamburg. Ossi was the only person in his family that survived.

Ossi Findling with Prince Charles
at a reception at St. James's Palace, 2007.

Courtesy of Ossi Findling, London, UK

MEMORIES THAT WON'T GO AWAY

Train 42

SUSANNE GOLDSMITH (NÉE WEISS)

Susanne was born in Vienna. She was seven years old when she and her brother Peter left on the first Kindertransport out of Vienna on December 10, 1938. Her father, Dr. Hans Weiss was an attorney for the Jewish community in Vienna. After Kristallnacht, he realized that there was no future for his family in Austria and immediately arranged for Susanne and Peter to go to England on the Kindertransport.

In England, after living in a hastily arranged camp for the refugee children, Susanne and Peter were interviewed by an English couple, Max and Sylvia Stone, who took them into their home that very same day. After they had settled in and felt comfortable, the Stones made a home for ten other refugee children. They were true heroes of the Kindertransport.

Courtesy of Susanne Goldsmith, Burbank, California, USA

E ve was born in Vienna on June 2, 1933. She arrived at Liverpool Street Station in London on a Kindertransport on April 27, 1939, when she was five years old. Her first foster home was with a Unitarian minister and his wife. They had no children and were very strict with her. A year later she went to another foster home in Cambridge, to a lovely loving family and remained with them for a few years. One of her uncles, a rabbi, was concerned that she was not in a Jewish environment, so she moved yet again to another family in Cambridge.

Her uncle and aunt had settled in West Hartlepool, northeast England. Eve visited them for a holiday. It was a wonderful turning point for her. Her aunt said, 'When you come back, you will be with us forever.' Eve was eleven years old and became one of their children.

Eve's mother was able to work and found employment in a factory. Tragically, the factory was bombed and her mother was killed just before the end of the war. Eve's father survived the war.

Eve later obtained a Ph.D. in biochemistry and worked as a researcher and biology teacher. She lives in London.

Courtesy of Eve Willman, London, UK

ROLF TAYLOR

BETTY ABRAMSON

RICHARD DREYFUS

GEORGE DREYFUS

Young German Jewish refugees en route to Australia on the *SS Orama*.

Photo courtesy of the United States Holocaust Memorial Museum

EVA KATE ANKER

DODI GRETTE ANKER

HILDE FOGELSON (NÉE ANKER)

Eva, Dodi and Hilde were three sisters, all born in Berlin. Eve was born in 1922, Dodi in 1924 and Hilde on May 29, 1926. Their parents were Georg and Gertrud (née Gottschalk) Anker. All three sisters were sent to safety in England by their parents on a Kindertransport that arrived on June 14, 1939. On July 13, 1939, their parents flew to Copenhagen, Denmark, where they stayed briefly before joining the sisters in England. In October 1940 the family sailed to the United States aboard the *SS Nova Scotia* and settled in Van Nuys, California.

Courtesy Hilde Fogelson and her son George Fogelson,
Los Angeles, California, USA

HEINZ B. KARPLUS

Heinz (Henry) was born in Berlin. He was a cousin of Eva, Dodi and Hilde Anker. In March 1939 Heinz and his sister Else left on a Kindertransport to England. Their parents joined them there before the war began. After the war Heinz immigrated to Chicago and Else and her parents remained in England.

Courtesy of George Fogelson, Los Angeles, California, USA

MARTIN TEICH-BIRKEN

Martin was born in Berlin in May 1922. His parents, Isaak David Birken and Martha (née Eichner) were both Polish immigrants to Germany. They married in 1910. Martin had three siblings, Adele, Saul and Lottie. Isaak and Martha also had a first son who died as a baby. After serving in World War I in the Austrian Army, Martin's father began the manufacture of men's clothing. Adele and Saul attended the Lyceum-Gymnasium School and Lotte took up an apprenticeship as a milliner. Martin's father acquired German citizenship in 1927. Saul left for the United States in April 1938. Lotte and Adele came to England to work in domestic service in December 1938 and March 1939, respectively.

Martin was too old, by three months, to be eligible to go on a Kindertransport and had to obtain a trainee permit, a British transit visa (with guarantors in America) and deposit the sum of £100 to Bloomsbury House in London, which he obtained from an uncle in Belgium. Although his sisters had obtained a British entry permit for him, he did not want to leave until the emigration of his parents was secured. On August 10, they received boat tickets to Cuba and he left the same evening, travelling to his uncle in Belgium and on to London on August 24, 1939, just a few days before war was declared.

However, his parents were in the first deportation of Jews from Berlin to the Lodz Ghetto, Poland, on October 18, 1941, and from there, in the first transport to the Chelmo extermination camp in January 1942.

Photo and text courtesy of the Jewish Museum, London, UK

GRETE RUDKIN (NÉE GLAUBER)

Grete was born in Vienna in 1930. In 1939 her mother Elsa sent her on a Kindertransport to England. A friend of the family helped to make the necessary arrangements. Like thousands of Jewish children from across Austria, Germany and Czechoslovakia, Grete took the train to Holland and then a ferry to England.

Photo courtesy of the Jewish Museum, London, UK

TOM GRAUMANN

Tom lived in a little village outside of the country district of Brno called Tesany before he left on a 'Winton train' in August 1939. Upon arrival in England Tom went by train to Selkirk, where he met many Czech children waiting for their Scottish families to collect them. From there he went to Dunbar for two-three weeks. The father of the family he stayed with was later called up to the army and the family lost their home, so Tom could no longer stay with them. He spent the rest of his time in Scotland living with a lady called Mary Corson, who had a home in a village near the town of Oban in the Western Highlands of Scotland.

Tom's mother and brother died in Sobibor.

Courtesy of Tom Graumann, Czech Republic

MARGOT GOLDSTEIN

Margot was one of a number of German Jewish refugee children who went to the safe haven of Australia on the passenger ship *SS Orama*.

United States Holocaust Memorial Museum,
courtesy of Dr. Glen Palmer

DAVE LUX (FORMERLY ISIDOR PINKASOVICH)

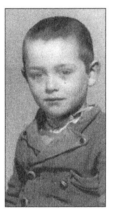

Dave was born in a small town near Bratislava in April 1933. On March 15, 1939, one month before his sixth birthday, Dave and his older brother Yaacov left their parents and were taken to Prague. They remained there until arrangements had been secured for them to leave on a Kindertransport from Prague Main railway station. They traveled via Holland and then by boat and train, arriving at Liverpool Street Station in London on April 19, 1939. Both boys were assigned to the Jewish Boys' Home in Ely, near Cambridge. They spent the next ten years there, not knowing if they had any living family members. Later, they learned their parents had perished in Auschwitz.

In 1949, shortly after the establishment of the State of Israel, Dave and his brother immigrated there with Youth Aliyah. They worked on Kibbutz Sa'ad, which is about twenty-eight miles from Be'er Sheva. Soon they heard from their father's sister, a Holocaust survivor, who was living in the United States in Brooklyn. She was anxious that they should both join her. Yaacov remained in Israel; Dave decided to go.

About eight months later, Dave moved to Cleveland to relatives that he discovered were living there. Soon after he settled in Cleveland, he met his future wife Helene. They married one year later and went to Los Angeles for their honeymoon. They both liked it so much they decided to settle there. Dave and Helene have been married for fifty-two years and have three children and five grandchildren.

Dave is a public speaker who frequently accepts speaking

engagements in religious institutions, law enforcement agencies, public organizations, schools, colleges and universities. He dedicates every talk he gives to his parents, because he was never able to thank them for their courage and bravery.

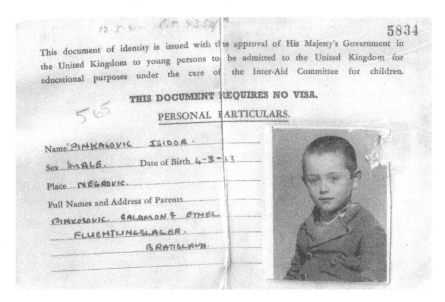

Courtesy of Dave Lux, Los Angeles, California, USA

HEBREW CLASSES IN ENGLAND

Jewish refugee children attending Hebrew classes.

United States Holocaust Memorial Museum, courtesy of Fay Cohen Stein

MARTHA BLEND (NÉE IMMERDAUER)

Martha was born in Vienna in 1930 and left on a Kindertransport to England in 1939. She spent the war with her Jewish foster parents, moving about to avoid the Blitz and adapting to a new life and a new language. After graduating from London University in 1951, she trained as a teacher, married and had two sons. She retired in 1990 after twenty-five years as a teacher. She now does voluntary work at the Holocaust Survivor Centre; she is a speaker in schools and colleges and has written a number of articles about her experiences.

Text extracts from A Child Alone *by Martha Blend.*
Courtesy of Martha Blend, London, UK

CHANITA RODNEY (NÉE ANNELISE CHARLOTTE LOWI)

Chanita was born in Berlin in July 1929. Shortly after Kristallnacht in 1938, Chanita was abducted and abused for several weeks at the hands of some Hitler youth. Her older brother Hanns rescued her and brought her home from this terrible ordeal that she had been forced to endure. Her father was devastated by what she had gone through and was determined to find a safe haven for both his children. Soon after her return, her parents had both Chanita and her brother dressed in their very best clothes to have a picture taken, which was sent to relatives abroad in the hope of finding a sponsor that would take them both. The photo attracted the Levys, who had no children of their own, but decided to take just Chanita. Her brother would have to remain behind.

She was ten years old when her father left her abruptly at a railway station, after putting a suitcase in her hand. He watched her and all the other children with nametags hanging around their necks board the Kindertransport to England.

Chanita was brought up by Mr. and Mrs. Levy, who lived in

Liverpool. She remembers clearly the tremendous adjustments that she had to make for a new life in a strange country. She constantly worried about the fate of her parents and her brother. She later learned that her brother was not saved. He and her family were sent from Berlin to Theresienstadt in 1942 and then in 1944 to Auschwitz. Her brother died in a Dachau hospital just five weeks before liberation.

Chanita completed her school years in Liverpool and excelled in her studies. Mrs. Levy made plans for her to advance to college education but she was determined to go to Palestine. In 1947, much against the Levys' wishes, she went to the *Hachshara* farm in Sussex where she met her future husband, Bob Rodney (formerly Rudi Reutner, a Jewish refugee from Hamburg, Germany). He had spent years as a British soldier.

In March 1949, after a three-month delay staying in Marseilles, France, Chanita arrived in Israel. Bob, who had left England several months earlier, was there to meet her and take her to their new home in Kibbutz Kfar Ha'Nasi. They were married in May 1950. Three of their children were born in Kibbutz Kfar Ha'Nasi. The fourth child was born in Timorim, a *moshav* (farm cooperative) in the south of Israel.

Rina, one of Chanita's cherished children, was showing signs of troubling behavioral patterns and this began a very long and tough road until her behavior was diagnosed as schizophrenia. Chanita was determined that this diagnosis should not be with any stigma or shame because there is no shame, just ignorance when misunderstood. She studied and read as much as she could about the neuro-bio-chemical brain disease of schizophrenia. With this information, she set about educating the public at large and spreading awareness that proper treatment of this disease can allow a loved one to lead a normal life. She was determined that no other family should ever be allowed again to go through the suffering that her family did.

In 1977 she established *Enosh* (the Hebrew term for human), the Israel Mental Health Association. It is aimed not only at public education and support but also the promotion of research on mind-related diseases. Chanita has received enormous recognition and numerous awards as a result of her many years of dedication and determination. In November 2012 the Hebrew University of Jerusalem bestowed on her an honorary doctorate for founding *Enosh* and for establishing a fund for brain research at the university.

Chanita has received many awards as the Founder-President of *Enosh*. Today she continues as a public speaker both locally and internationally and has been awarded many prestigious prizes over the years and gained international acclaim.

Chanita's autobiography *The Gift of Life* details her life and her accomplishments.

Courtesy of Chanita Rodney, Hon. PhD, Kfar Saba, Israel

HERMANN HIRSCHBERGER

Hermann was born in Karlsruhe, western Germany in July 1926. After Kristallnacht Hermann's family found it impossible to obtain refuge as a family, so they decided to enroll Hermann and his brother on the Kindertransport. Both boys left home in 1939 accompanied by their father, who went with them as far as Hamburg. From there, the boys boarded the liner *SS Manhattan*. They arrived in Southampton in March 1939. Both parents perished in Auschwitz in 1942, having made the courageous decision that their children should be saved.

Hermann celebrated his Bar Mitzvah in a refugee hostel run by the B'nai B'rith in Cliftonville, a seaside town in southeast England. In the spring of 1940 he was evacuated and given lodgings with a coalmining family in Staffordshire. At the age of fifteen and living in a hostel in London, he began work in a north London factory, which manufactured diesel fuel-injection pumps for submarines. He continued his education in evening classes, where he matriculated to become a design draftsman with a machine tool company.

He continued to attend evening classes for the next seven years. He became a chartered engineer and joined Smiths Industries, then Elliot Automation, and in 1968 he joined Kodak, where he stayed for twenty-one years. He rose through the ranks to become manager of the development department, managing a staff of ninety.

In 1962 Hermann married Eva, the daughter of refugees who had settled in Brazil. They have two children and four grandchildren. He retired in 1989 and then did only voluntary work, and his communal responsibilities expanded. He was a founding member of Belmont Synagogue and has been an Employment Resource Center advisor, a school governor and a Young Enterprise advisor for Harrow. After visiting Karlsruhe in 1988, where he addressed German schoolchildren, he was invited to share his experiences in synagogues, at JACS (Jewish Association of Cultural Studies) and especially in schools where he frequently gives talks.

Hermann was elected Chairman of the KT-AJR in 2003. At the dedication of the Kindertransport statue outside Liverpool Street Station, he was the spokesperson on behalf of the *kinder*. One of the highlights during his chairmanship was an invitation, together with one hundred other members of the Kindertransport Group, to meet Prince Charles and the Duchess of Cornwall at Clarence House as part of the celebrations for the 60th anniversary of the ending of World War II, at which he spoke eloquently on behalf of his fellow Kindertransportees.

In January 2011 Hermann was awarded an MBE by the Queen in recognition for his services to the Jewish community and the Kindertransport evacuees.

Western Germany

Courtesy of HMD (Northwood Holocaust Memorial Day Events)

Train 44

CHILDREN ATTENDING A PURIM CARNIVAL

Children at the *Beith Ahawah* orphanage in Berlin attending a Purim[10] Carnival. Some children stayed at this orphanage before leaving on a Kindertransport.

United States Holocaust Memorial Museum, courtesy of Anna Leist

10. The festival of Purim is celebrated every year on the 14th day of the Hebrew month of Adar (late winter/early spring). It commemorates the salvation of the Jewish people in ancient Persia from Haman's plot 'to destroy, kill and annihilate all the Jews, young and old, infants and women, in a single day'.

FRITZ BARSCHAK

F ritz was born in Vienna in March 1931. He left Vienna on a Kindertransport in December 1938.

Courtesy of Pearl and Graham Aaronson, London, UK

ERICA STEINBERGER (NÉE ERIKA LÖBL)

WERNER LOVAL (FORMERLY LÖBL)

Excerpted from Werner M. Loval,
We Were Europeans: A Personal History of a Turbulent Century.

I n mid-June 1939, Erika and I left our family's home at 27 Luitpoldstrasse [in Bamberg, Germany] for the last time.

Erika and I drove with our parents to Würzburg, where we said goodbye. Then, Erika 'Sarah' Löbl, aged 15, and Werner 'Israel' Löbl, aged 13, carrying travel documents stamped with a large red 'J,' joined the *Kindertransport* and boarded the train for Bremen and the SS *Europa* on our way out of Nazi Germany.

Vera Simonis, who worked for one of the Jewish refugee committees set up to rescue German Jewish children, succeeded in finding a guarantor for Erika and me: Miss Ailsey Lazarus, a single lady from an aristocratic Jewish banking family in London, to whom, of course, we were perfect strangers. Miss Lazarus took upon herself the entire financial responsibility for both of us, including school fees and related expenses, the cost of vacations, and later even paid for our journey from England to Ecuador.

On August 1, 1940, at the eleventh hour, our parents finally escaped from Germany and on October 16, 1942, our family was reunited at last. From Erika's diary: 'Now, it still seems like a dream to me to sit here…with Daddy in the same house, and suddenly all the travel has come to an end. It is almost too much all at once.…

Our family in Bamberg, 1936

Everything seems like years ago, and when I think about it, the tears almost come to my eyes. But then there is the anticipation of Quito and Mummy, and everything that awaits us there.'

Years later, after our dear mother's death, we found the following insert among the pages of her prayer book:

Prayer of a Mother Separated from her Children

My children live in a distant land, far from their parents' home, far from their father's heart and their mother's care, and I, whose greatest joy should be to watch over their health, to protect every one of their steps, to embrace them with never-ending love and devotion – I am far from them; my eyes do not reach them, nor does my hand, and there is nothing I can do other than pray to You, my Lord, for their well-being and safety.

O hear my heart's fervent plea, take my children under Your almighty wings, with Your merciful hand lead them over every stone and thorn in their path, endow them with gifts of grace and kindness, together with wise and modest behavior with which they may win people's hearts and which may bring them kindness and goodwill in those hearts, so that cold, faraway lands may become as familiar to them as home and hearth.

Sustain them healthy and fit in body and spirit, shelter them from evil and wrongdoing, from harm and injury. Protect them from temptation and help them resist both temptations from without as well as the turmoil of inner passions so that these may never gain a hold over them; that their souls may remain pure and sincere and they may hold fast in childlike innocence and piety to all that is noble and Divine, that their eyes and faces may always be a reflection of their pure hearts.

Grant them, O Heavenly Father, strength and reason, perseverance and the will to understand their challenges, tasks, and obligations and to fulfill them with joy and love so that they may benefit from these and be blessed and be led to the summits of life and happiness. Help them overcome all obstacles and privations and grant them everything that can serve as a foundation for their present and future well-being.

Hear, O Father, my fervent, heartfelt prayer and may the time not be distant when You will return my children to me, full of life's vitality and happiness, to be my heart's pride and joy, with the blessings of mankind and the grace of God my Lord.

Amen.

Erika and I remained close friends with Miss Lazarus throughout

Werner with Ailsey Lazarus (left) and Vera Simonis-Downs in 1981 at Ms. Lazarus's house in Knightsbridge, London

the years and visited her often at her elegant townhouse in Knightsbridge, London. It is an indication of her great generosity that Miss Lazarus never agreed to our later offer to pay back the considerable sums she spent on our behalf. Ailsey Lazarus died on October 21, 1991, at age 92.

After living in England, Ecuador, and the United States, Werner made his home in Israel. Following an exciting career in Israel's diplomatic service in the US and Latin America, he initiated the development of Jerusalem's Nayot neighborhood in 1960 and established the now 65-branch Anglo-Saxon Real Estate Agency, of which he continues to be a partner. A founding member of the Har-El Reform Congregation in Jerusalem, he also played a major role in the birth of the Israel Movement for Progressive Judaism. He lives in Jerusalem with his wife, Pamela. They are the parents of two sons and two daughters, and grandparents of twelve.

Courtesy of Werner M. Loval, Jeruslaem, Israel

Train 45

MARGARET 'GRETEL' GOLDBERGER (NÉE HELLER)

Margaret was born in Berlin, in April 1926. Margaret was thirteen when she left on a Kindertransport to England in June 1939. In London she stayed with a family for a short while and then she went to a hostel run by the B'nai B'rith. She remained in England until after World War II, when she was reunited with her mother in New York.

Margaret is active in various Jewish organizations. She is a frequent speaker, primarily to students at the Nassau Country Holocaust and Tolerance Center. She is a member of the B'nai B'rith International Board of Governors and she is head of the Speakers Bureau of the Kindertransport Association. Margaret remains deeply involved in bringing people together that are associated with the Kindertransport.

Courtesy of Margaret Goldberger, Hicksville, New York, USA

LILLY SCHISCHA
CILLY HORWITZ
FRIEDA KOHN
THEA HERZBERG
ANITA SCHILLER
LOTTE LEVY

LILLY SCHISCHA
Born in Vienna

CILLY HORWITZ
Born in Hamburg

FRIEDA KOHN
Born in Berlin

THEA HERZBERG
Born in Dresden

ANITA SCHILLER
Born in Vienna

LOTTE LEVY
Born in Cologne

Six Jewish refugee girls who lived in the B'nai B'rith hostel in Hackney, London.

United States Holocaust Memorial Museum,
courtesy of Ruth Wassermann Segal

Train 46

HANNAH SCHMIDT

RUTH SCHMIDT

ELLEN SCHMIDT

Hannah, Ruth and Ellen were the daughters of Walter and Dora Schmidt. Hannah and Ellen left on a Kindertransport from Frankfurt to England. Their sister Ruth escaped from Germany, but not on a Kindertransport.

Courtesy of Ellen Silk, Sherman Oaks, California, USA

WALTER WETZMANN

Walter and his sister Eva left Vienna on a Kindertransport to France in March 1939.

United States Holocaust Memorial Museum,
courtesy of Eva Moore

EDDIE NUSSBAUM

Eddie was born in Hamburg, Germany. In April 1939, at the age of fifteen, he left on a Kindertransport to England. He worked as an apprentice in a London machine shop and attended night school in mechanical engineering. After the war broke out in September 1939, he became an 'enemy alien' and was interned in May 1940. Some 2500 such internees boarded the infamous troopship *Dunera* in July 1940 and were taken to Australia. After disembarking in Sydney, the internees were moved to a camp in Hay, New South Wales, and later to a camp at Tatura, Victoria. Eddie's release from internment came through early and he returned to England on the *Stirling Castle* as a free man in November 1941.

Eddie returned to his original machine shop in London and also to the part-time classes at the Polytechnic for his B.Sc. Engineering degree. Soon after the end of the war, he got his British citizenship and his London University engineering degree. He won a post-graduate fellowship in 1948 and spent all of 1949 in the United States studying steel mill practice. This led to a management job in the rolling mill field back in the USA. In 1950 he married his British girlfriend and they immigrated to New York. They had two children, Linda and David. In 1988 Eddie and Daphne moved to Los Angeles.

Hamburg, Harbour

Courtesy of Eddie Nussbaum, Los Angeles, California, USA

Train 47

INGRID WUGA (NÉE WOLFF)

Ingrid was born in Dortmund, Germany in 1924. Her parents were Ascher and Erna Wolff. From 1930-36 Ingrid attended primary school. After Kristallnacht, in November 1938, Ingrid's father was sent to the Buchenwald concentration camp. In 1939 the family moved to Hamburg. Ingrid attended a Jewish school and then worked as a trainee domestic at the Paulinenstift (Pauline Foundation) Orphanage in Hamburg. Shortly after that, in July 1939, Ingrid left on a Kindertransport to her guarantors – the Dixon family – in Ashby-de-la-Zouch, England. Not permitted to further her education, she was sent to work as a mother's help. Ingrid was reunited with her parents a couple of months later when they came to England as domestic servants.

Courtesy of Ingrid and Henry Wuga, Scotland, UK

Henry was born in Nuremberg, Germany in 1924. His parents were Karl and Lore Wuga. His primary school years began in 1930. The summers were spent in children's homes. In 1935-37 the Nuremberg racial laws came into full force with the persecution of Jews. Henry joined *Habonim Hachshara*. He left school in 1938 and followed his mother's suggestion for him to learn a trade. As the family had a catering background, Henry started as a commis chef in a kosher hotel in Baden-Baden.

In 1938, after Kristallnacht, Henry returned back home. His parents sent Henry on a Kindertransport to England in 1939. His guarantor was Mrs. E. Hurwich. She lived in Glasgow and gave him a wonderful welcome. In 1940 Henry was arrested and taken into custody for 'corresponding with the enemy.' He had sent letters to his parents via his uncles in Paris and Brussels – a serious offence in wartime – and he was declared a 'category A dangerous enemy alien' at the High Court in Edinburgh. He spent ten months in a series of internment camps, ending up on the Isle of Man. Further tribunals regarded him as a 'friendly alien' and he was released because 'he was under age to be interned'.

From 1941-44 Henry returned to Glasgow where he worked in many quality restaurants and hotels as a chef de partie. He married Ingrid Wolff, who had also been a Kindertransportee. He became very active in German/Austrian refugee clubs. He became a British citizen.

Henry and his wife Ingrid enjoy a busy retirement with their family and grandsons. They are immensely proud to have been honored by Her Majesty the Queen in 1999 at an investiture ceremony at the Palace of Holyroodhouse in Edinburgh, Scotland, where he was presented with an MBE for his work with the British Limbless Ex-Servicemen's Association.

Nuremberg, Germany

Courtesy of Ingrid and Henry Wuga, Scotland, UK

ERNEST O. WEINMAN

(formerly Ernst O. Weinmann)

Ernest was fifteen when he left Vienna on a Kindertransport in June 1939. He arrived at Harwich two days later. In the fall of 1940 Ernest came to the United States.

Courtesy of Hans Weinmann,
W. Bloomfield, Michigan, USA

HANS R. WEINMANN

Hans, Ernest's younger brother, was thirteen when he left Vienna on a Kindertransport in June 1939. He arrived at Harwich two days later. Hans came to the United States on June 1, 1940.

Courtesy of Hans Weinmann,
W. Bloomfield, Michigan, USA

ROSIE SCHEINMANN

Rosie was born in 1928 in Berlin. Her parents were Moshe and Lotte Scheinmann. Rosie left on a Kindertransport from Berlin to England in 1939.

Courtesy of Daniella Gold,
New York, New York, USA

ADI (ADOLF) SCHEINMANN

Adi was born in Berlin in 1924. He came to England on one of the last Kindertransports from Berlin in August 1939.

Courtesy of Daniella Gold,
New York, New York, USA

KURT STERN

HARRY STERN

Kurt and Harry were the sons of Moses Stern and Selma Rosenberger-Stern. Kurt was born in Bratislava in April 1928 and Harry was born in Bratislava in November 1930. In May 1939 Kurt and Harry left on a Kindertransport to England.

Slovak National Theater,
Bratislava, Slovakia

United States Holocaust Memorial Museum, courtesy of Max Stern

JOSEPH HABERER

LUTZ GOLDNER

BENJAMIN BAMBERGER

HENRY DUCKSTEIN

WERNER COHN

Five Jewish refugee boys who arrived in England on a Kindertransport in 1939
pose for a photograph outside a synagogue in Nottingham, England.

*United States Holocaust Memorial Museum,
courtesy of Mordechai Vered*

FRIEDEL SCHECTER

Friedel was a young Jewish refugee who arrived in England on a Kindertransport. She studied at the Whittingehame *Hachshara*.

Courtesy of the United States Holocaust Memorial Museum

KATE LESSER

Kate was born in Prague. Very soon after her arrival in England on a Kindertransport, she was sent to the Stoatley Rough Boarding School that was run by refugees in Haslemere, in the south of England. Kate stayed at the school until April 1946, when she left for the United States.

United States Holocaust Memorial Museum, courtesy Bernard Kelly

HERMAN GOLD

Herman was a young German Jewish refugee who went to Australia on the *SS Orama*. This ship was built in 1924 for the Orient Line and had accommodation for 1,700 passengers. The *SS Orama* was converted to a troopship in 1940 and was used to transport the British Expeditionary Force to Norway following the German invasion.

United States Holocaust Memorial Museum, courtesy Dr. Glen Palmer

GERALD HEUMANN

(formerly Gerhard Heumann)

Gerald was born in Hirschaid, Germany, on July 3, 1926. He left Germany on his own after his mother's papers were ripped up by the SS. His father died when he was two years old. Reports suggest that his mother remarried. Her last known destination with her husband was Buchenwald. Gerald arrived on a Kindertransport to England around June 21, 1939. He lived in London with an aunt and uncle. During the war he was evacuated. He returned to London after the war. His wife Frances was from England. Gerald died on June 1, 2009.

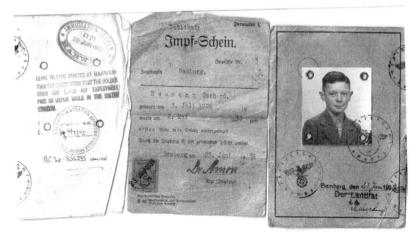

Courtesy of Gary Heumann, London, UK

Margit was born in January 1922. In June 1939 Margit left Prague on one of the Winton transports – Transport Label No. 7726. When she arrived at Liverpool Street Station in London, she was met by a Quaker lady who took her and another young girl on a sightseeing trip around London before putting them on a train to Glasgow, Scotland. Margit went to live with the Grossman family in Pollokshields, a district of Glasgow, as a domestic/servant for a few months before the family was evacuated from Glasgow due to the fear of the city being bombed. Margit went to live and work as an untrained nurse in a hospital in a very rough part of Glasgow until she moved to London. In 1947 she married Geoffrey Goodman, who became a renowned journalist. They had a son and daughter.

Jenty	5172	3. 7.27	- as above. C.T.Hostel.	Czech Section	Czech Section	
Tomas	1823	31. 7.26	Edmonton Castle nr Carlisle.	Rosina M. Philp, Renee, The Grove, Clacton on Sea.	Czech Section	
Hanna	5886	29.11.30	N.Staffs.Committee Hostel, Stoke/Trent.	N.Staffs.Committee.	Czech Section	
G Margit	7726	29. 1.22	c/o Norman Grossman, 18 Melville Street, Pollokshields,Glasgow.	Movement.	Movement.	Permi throu Movem
Fritz	1725	6. 7.29	With guarantor	Rev.Edwin Keling, 13 High St,Old Basford Nottingham.	Personal guarantee	
Peter Bedrich	12387	8. 5.26	c/o {Moravian Church Board, 32 Fetter Lane,E.C.4.} Moravian School for Boys, Fulneck, Leeds.	Moravian Church Board, 32 Fetter Lane, E.C.4.	Bank Guarantee	
H Julius	1820	7. 6.27	Rugby Cttee. Hostel.	M. Daniels, North Western Hospital, Lawn Road, N.W.3.	Czech Section	
Pavel	12388	23. 2.25	King's School House, Macclesfield, Ches.	Thos. Taylor Shaw, Kings School House, Macclesfield, Ches.	Bank guarantee	At Kin House,
ELD Gerhard	1647	17. 9.24	Mana Farm Tilgrith Beds.	Movement.	Youth Aliyah.	At You farm a

Margit Goodman on the Winton Train list.

Courtesy of Karen Goodman, London, UK

Train 50

GERARD FRIEDENFELD

Gerard was fourteen when he arrived on a Kindertransport at London's Liverpool Street Station from Prague, with 135 other Jewish children aged two to fifteen years of age.

United States Holocaust Memorial Museum, courtesy of Gerard Friedenfeld

Joe was born in Vienna in 1928. He was raised in Czechoslovakia and lived in the center of Bratislava, the capital of Slovakia. His parents were amongst those who desperately tried to get their children out to safety. He and his younger brother Ernie took English lessons from a young lady in preparation for their departure to England. In July 1939, when Joe was eleven and his brother Ernie was nine, they left for England. As they were coming from Slovakia, they were not permitted to join the transport in Prague. Therefore they had to wait for the train from Prague in Lovosice, a border town inside the German Reich. The train was running late and it was getting dark. The German official in charge of the railroad station insisted they went inside the building. In Hitler's Germany, however, Jews were not permitted in the waiting rooms, so they were escorted into the men's toilet. Joe spent his final moments with his father in a lavatory in the German Reich!

The atmosphere in the train was mixed. Some children, including his brother Ernie, were crying. For some of the others, going to England was an exciting adventure. When they left Germany and entered Holland they received a welcome cup of hot cocoa and bread. When they arrived at the port of the Hook of Holland they boarded a big ship. That night they crossed the English Channel. The following morning they arrived at London's Liverpool Street Station. The first night in London, Joe and Ernie stayed in someone's home – it was not until many years later that Joe learned that this 'someone's home' was Nicholas Winton's mother's home.

In 1941 Joe joined the Czechoslovak boarding school in Wales. Ernie followed him. They spent four very happy years there. One of his responsibilities at the school was to review the daily news headlines. This is when Joe was first introduced to journalism.

After the war Joe returned as quickly as possible to Prague. He was deeply concerned about the fate of his parents. He went to a dedicated center where families that had been torn apart were able to try and find each other. Inside the building, the walls were covered with lists of names but there was no trace of his parents. Much later, he learned that his parents had been deported by the Nazis to Poland. To this day, he does not know how they perished.

Joe started his journalistic career in 1948 in the Prague bureau of the Associated Press. When the communists took over in Czechoslovakia and started arresting AP staffers, he fled across the Iron Curtain to Austria and in 1950 came to Canada. He started working on construction jobs in Vancouver and on B.C. coastal ships. In 1951 he enrolled at the University of British Columbia. One day, he walked into the editorial offices of the University's student newspaper *Ubyssey* and was offered a job. That was the real beginning of his career as an extraordinary journalist. Since that day, journalism has taken Joe to every corner of the world.

Joe has been honored a number of times for his journalism. He has won four Gemini awards, the John Drainie award for distinguished contribution to Canadian broadcasting and a Hot Doc award for documentary writing. He was awarded honorary doctorates by the University of British Columbia, the Royal Military College and Dalhousie University. He has also received a Lifetime Achievement Award from the Canadian Journalism Foundation.

Photos courtesy of the archive of Joe Schlesinger
and courtesy of Matej Mináč – The Lottery of Life

Franz was born in Breslau, Germany, in June 1927. The following year, his family moved to Ratibor (now Raciborz) and remained there for nine years when his father, Dr. Richard Krebs, a decorated World War I veteran, retired his judgeship. The family returned to Breslau, soon after which Dr. Krebs was arrested and sent to Buchenwald. He remained there for four weeks but was released along with other prisoners who were World War I veterans. During his imprisonment the Jewish community of Breslau drew up a list of ten children to be sent to Great Britain on the first Kindertransport. Preference was given to children whose fathers had been imprisoned. Because of this, and the help from an elderly aunt who was present when the children were chosen, Franz was included on the list and sent to England via Berlin and Antwerp. Shortly after his arrival in England, he was sent to the Dovercourt Bay camp.

Franz's family fled from Breslau to England, where they remained until the end of the war. Franz graduated from the New Herrlingen School in Wem, Shropshire, England, in June 1944. After the war he returned with his family to Germany to study architecture. In 1956 he immigrated to the United States.

Breslau, Germany

Text courtesy of the United States Holocaust Memorial Museum,
courtesy of Franz Werner

Train 51

CHILDREN ARRIVING AT HARWICH

Berta Baczeles and her brother Josef left Vienna in December 1938 on a Kindertransport. They arrived in Hull, in the northeast of England, two days later. Berta was eight years old and her brother was thirteen.

The following depicts the entire group of children who arrived on that train. They are pictured on the platform at Harwich Station (on the southeast coast of England) before changing trains to go to Hull, their final destination.

Hull Jewish Committee for Refugees

Children arriving at Harwich en route for Hull via Dovercourt holiday camp,
December 2, 1938, from Vienna, Bremen and Berlin

Accompanied by

Mrs. D.M. Rosen and Mr. Philip Bloom.

| Berta Baczeles | Walter Sobolka | Josef Baczeles | Eva L. Burstyn | Tilde Burstyn | Herbert Burstyn | Fritz Barschak |

Others: Ruth Lindenfeld, Edith Urmacher, Gertrud Hirschenhauer, Gerda Urmacher,
Helene Stern, Ruth Meier, Ursula Koerbchen, Ellen Auster, Ursel Gutermann,
Kurt Markstein, Norbet and Beile Eisen, Walter Glossau, Karl Heilbrunn

Researcher: Jack Lennard, Hull, UK
Photo and text information courtesy of Pearl and Graham Aaronson, London, UK

Train 52

KENNETH LOWE (FORMERLY KURT LÖWENSTEIN)

RUDI LÖWENSTEIN

Kenneth (Kurt) was born on September 6, 1923, in Düsseldorf, Germany. He left Düsseldorf on a Kindertransport to London on April 19, 1939. Unbeknownst to him, he traveled on the same transport as his future wife Margaret 'Gretel', who he was to meet two years later in Birmingham, UK.

Rudi was born on July 21, 1921, in Düsseldorf. He left there on a Kindertransport to London in February 1939 and later moved to Winnipeg, Canada. Rudi married and had three boys.

Courtesy of David Lowe and Susan Mann,
Brookline, Massachusetts, USA

MARGARET LOWE

(née Margarete 'Gretel' Pappenheimer)

Margarete 'Gretel' was born on September 12, 1922, in Munich, Germany. At midnight on April 18, 1939, she left Munich on a Kindertransport to England. Margaret and her husband Kenneth (Kurt) met two years later. She remembered him from the Kindertransport journey – he had joined the same transport as her, one day later from Düsseldorf. They married and settled in New York. Margaret's son David met Curtis Mann's daughter, Susan Mann in 2000 and later learned that three of their parents left Germany on the very same Kindertransport train in April 1939. Susan and David married in 2002.

Courtesy of David Lowe and Susan Mann,
Brookline, Massachusetts, USA

CURTIS MANN (FORMERLY ZUCKERMAN)

Curtis was born on March 3, 1926, in Frankfurt. He left Germany on April 19, 1939, on a Kindertransport to England. Several months later, his mother, the late Martha Slotkin, joined him in England. Soon after, in 1941, they boarded a boat bound for the United States to join his older brother Harvey, who had already made the journey and was living in Cape Girardeau, Missouri. After finishing school, Curtis, his mother and brother moved to St. Louis.

In his later years, Curtis spent time working with various charitable organizations, including the Kindertransport Association, for which he volunteered to give lectures to children about his early experiences escaping the Holocaust. He also worked with B'nai B'rith, *Mazon* (a Jewish organization that fights global hunger) and the St. Louis Foodbank.

Courtesy of David Lowe and Susan Mann,
Brookline, Massachusetts, USA

Elizabeth was born in June 1922 in Fuerth, northern Bavaria, in Germany. When she was very young, her family moved to Nuremberg. The looting of the family apartment during Kristallnacht, combined with the increase in danger of just being Jewish, led her father and mother to apply for, and get, a space for Elizabeth on a Kindertransport from Nuremberg to London in June 1939, on the eve of her seventeenth birthday. While in London, she worked in the household of the Frankels, taking care of their two little boys and doing housework. Elizabeth and Joyce Frankel started a correspondence that continued until Joyce's death, almost seventy years later.

When she was moved from London, Elizabeth lived and worked in a number of locations. She always recalls living in Tunbridge Wells, where she worked as a nurses' aide in a big country home set up to accommodate the infant evacuees from the major cities. As the war continued, and her many attempts to help her family stalled, an opportunity for Elizabeth to join her sister Margaret in New York presented itself and she took it.

Elizabeth arrived in New York in the fall of 1940. She lived in Brooklyn before moving to the 92nd Street Y in Manhattan. Elizabeth worked in the fashion industry, for both Elizabeth Arden and Mainbocher. Elizabeth met her future husband David Goldfarb, a New York native, at the Y. They had two daughters: Rachel, born 1951, and Miriam, born 1954. The family moved to Stamford, Connecticut, in September 1959. Elizabeth and David operated a ladies sportswear shop in Greenwich, Connecticut, until 1969. They then opened a jewelry gallery stocked with their own creations and Elizabeth's antique jewelry collections, which remained open until 1996. In retirement Elizabeth remained an active supporter of numerous charities, until a brain injury limited her activities. She still lives in Stamford.

Sketch of Elizabeth

Courtesy of Miriam Goldfarb, Stamford, Connecticut, USA

Charlotte was born in Danzig (Gdansk), Poland. She was eleven years old when she arrived in England on a Kindertransport.

Charlotte is the girl on the right in the back row.
The photograph was taken in England in 1940.

Photo courtesy of Charlotte Kapp, Boca Raton, Florida, USA

Train Fifty-Two

227

Train 53

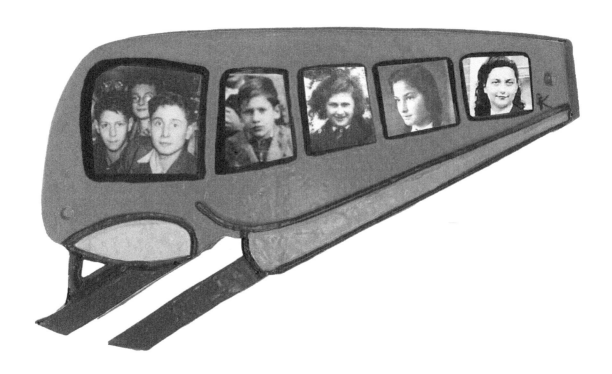

GERHARD GLASS

Gerhard was was sent to France on a Kindertransport in the spring of 1939 and stayed at the Quincy-sous-Senart children's home near Paris.

United States Holocaust Memorial Museum,
courtesy of Stephan H. Lewy

SUSI BRADFIELD (NÉE NEUWIRTH)

Susi was born in Berlin on December 23, 1929. She left on the Kindertransport with her sister Paula on January 18, 1939. They lived in Gateshead and Sunderland until their parents and younger brother arrived, just before the war. The family then lived for a few years in Sunderland in a rented house before moving to London in 1943. Susi married Freddie Bradfield, a refugee from Vienna, in 1949 and they settled in London, where they lived all their lives. They had three children: Michael, Vita and Cheryl, and four grandchildren. Sadly, their daughter Vita passed away when she was just three years old. Susi and Freddie died several years ago. Susi wrote a detailed story of her journey from Berlin to London in her book *But Some Became Stars*.

Courtesy of Mindy Wiesenberg, London, UK

ERICH ALTBUCH

HANS ALTBUCH

Erich and Hans, who were twins, were born in Vienna in February 1925. They left on a Kindertransport from Berlin through the Netherlands on December 1, 1938. Pictured with them is Sol Muller, who came from the Jewish Orphanage, Berlin-Pankow.

Photo courtesy of The Wiener Library for the Study of the Holocaust & Genocide, London, UK

GERDA ALEXANDRA WIESENBERG

(née Mathiason)

Gerda was born in Hamburg, Germany, on March 26, 1921. She left on a Kindertransport from Hamburg to England with her two sisters in December 1938 and arrived at Liverpool Street Station. After some time, they went to a Jewish hostel in Harrogate, where they stayed for a number of years. Their father managed to escape from Germany before the war and came to Leeds in northern England. Their mother stayed behind to sort out family business matters. She did not manage to leave and died in Theresienstadt. Gerda met her husband Zoli (Lazar Zoltan) Wiesenberg in Harrogate and they married in 1946. He was a refugee from Kosice, Czechoslovakia, and arrived in the UK in 1939. He served in the British Army in India during the war. They had two sons, David and Johnny, and eight grandchildren.

Courtesy of Mindy Wiesenberg, London, UK

PAULA RACKER (NÉE NEUWIRTH)

Paula was born in Berlin on May 31, 1927. She left on a Kindertransport with her sister Susi on January 18, 1939. After arriving in London, they went to Gateshead in northern England and spent two months with a Jewish family before moving to nearby Sunderland, where they stayed with another Jewish family. Their parents managed to get out of Germany with their younger brother Myer just before the war and they eventually joined them in Sunderland. In 1943 the family all moved to London and lived in Hampstead for a number of years. Their older brother Siche had already come to London some years earlier and was studying in Gateshead.

Paula married Zeev Racker, a Holocaust survivor from Poland, in 1952, after meeting him while she was on a visit to Israel in 1950. Zeev sadly passed away in 1992. Paula and Zeev had three daughters, Zena, Mindy and Dina, all named after his three sisters who perished in the Holocaust. They are married with children and Paula has many great-grandchildren.

Courtesy of Mindy Wiesenberg, London, UK

Train 54

RENATA LAXOVA (NÉE RENATE POLGAR)

Renata was born in July 1931 in Brno, Czechoslovakia. She left on a Kindertransport from Prague to England at the end of July 1939. She spent seven years in England and has always remained in close contact with the family who took her in. After the war she returned to Czechoslovakia and was one of the few children whose parents had survived. Renata has written two books about her experiences: the first, called *Letter to Alexander,* was published in English in 2001 (Custom Editorial Productions), the second, in Czech, was published in 2010 (Barrister & Principal, Brno, Czech Republic). She married Tibor Lax, a veterinarian. In 1968 Renata left Czechoslovakia again for England, this time with her husband and their two daughters. They have one grandchild.

The family has lived in Madison, Wisconsin, since 1975. Renata is now retired from the University of Wisconsin School of Medicine and Public Health.

Courtesy of Renata Laxova, Madison, Wisconsin, USA

Bob was born in Hanover, Germany in 1925. He was the youngest of three children. His father's family had been cattle dealers in southern Germany for generations. He can trace his family tree back to about 1700. His father went to school in Heidelberg and then he studied textiles in Frankfurt. His parents married in 1912 and settled in his mother's hometown of Hanover, where his father established a textile business. Bob's early childhood was comfortable and he started school in 1930. When the Nazis came to power in 1933, everything changed. When Bob started secondary education in 1936, his classmates were under orders not to associate with Jews – and usually the Jews were made to sit at the back and not participate in the lesson.

The question of emigration was often discussed; people were leaving continually but Bob's father resisted the idea for a long time. He had fought in World War I with some distinction and, like many others, thought this would count for something and keep them safe. Bob's sister, eleven years older than he, left for South Africa in 1936. Eventually his parents started to try to find ways of leaving. They made many applications, but all were refused.

After Kristallnacht, in November 1938, it became clear to all the Jewish community that they were in immediate danger. On May 3, 1939, at the age of thirteen, Bob left Hanover and traveled to England on a Kindertransport via Holland. At his first stop, inside the Dutch border, he was met by such kindness. People offered drinks and food and smiles. It was the first time for a long while that he had been greeted or offered a smile from anyone outside of his own immediate family. Bob's transport went to Liverpool Street Station. He and the other young children were taken to a large underground hall, where they all sat patiently with labels round their necks, waiting to be collected.

Up until the outbreak of war, he and his parents were able to stay in close contact. That soon changed. They were restricted to 25-word messages once a month via the Red Cross. Those messages stopped in 1941, and after the war he found out that his parents had been on the first transport out of Hanover, on December 15, 1941, to a concentration camp in Riga, Latvia. They never returned.

Bob met his wife Ann, another child of the Kindertransport, at a club for young Jewish refugees run by Woburn House. They were married May 21, 1950. Today, both Bob and Ann work tirelessly to raise awareness of the Holocaust and the experience of the Kindertransport through speaking at activities for Holocaust Memorial Day and throughout the rest of the year. They have two sons and three grandchildren.

Text extracts courtesy of Northwood Holocaust Memorial Day Events,
Northwood, UK

ANN KIRK

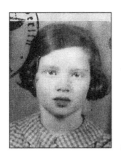

Ann was born in Berlin in 1928. In the mid-1930s she was still at a state school. She vividly remembers this time: Jews were not allowed to sit on park benches, go to swimming pools, the theatre or cinema, and gradually Jewish people were deprived of their rights as citizens. Ann's father went to retrain as a chiropodist/masseur, as he thought it would make it easier for the family to emigrate if he had a profession rather than being a businessman. Her mother found a job some 300 miles away from Berlin and Ann and her mother lived close to her job for about six months. When her father qualified, Ann and her mother rejoined him in Berlin in September 1938. He was only allowed to take Jewish patients and had a rubber stamp that said: 'Chiropodist to the Jews'.

It was difficult to find accommodation for Jews in Berlin but the family was able to live with a cousin of Ann's mother who worked as a caretaker to a Jewish school and had a spare room. On Kristallnacht Ann was awoken by her parents and cousins rushing about. They wouldn't tell her what was wrong. The following day Ann's parents told her that they had to pack a bag and leave immediately. What a sight it was: policemen and Nazis jeering while Jews swept up the glass and boarded windows. Synagogues were on fire. That evening the family went to stay with Ann's mother's best friend. After a while, things settled down a little and they were able to find a place to live. In Britain the idea of the Kindertransport had been hastily formulated. Synagogue congregations were asked to consider taking in children from across Europe. It was soon agreed that Ann would be looked after by two sisters who were social workers in the East End of London. Letters were exchanged and photographs sent.

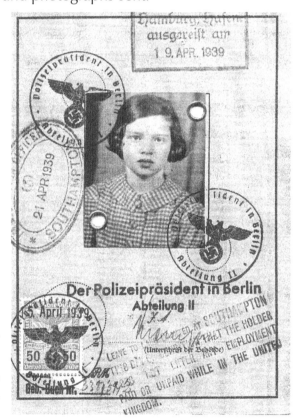

Ann's name came up on the Kindertransport list in April 1939. Her parents took her to the railway station where she saw many other parents and children in tears. As the train passed through the station, Ann saw her parents for the last time. She boarded an American ship in Hamburg and arrived in Southampton two days later.

Ann and her husband Bob, another child of the Kindertransport, married on May 21, 1950. They both work tirelessly to raise awareness of the Holocaust and the experience of the Kindertransport through speaking engagements throughout the year. They have two sons and three grandchildren.

Courtesy of HMD (Northwood Holocaust Memorial Day Events)
Northwood, Middlesex, UK

RUTH DOSWALD (NÉE HANNES)

R uth was born in Hamburg, Germany. She left on a Kindertransport to England in March 1939. She was ten years old.

Ruth in her brand new school uniform, taken two months after arriving in England.

Courtesy of Ruth Doswald

SUSI PODGURSKI (NÉE COHN)

Susi was born in Berlin. In 1939 she arrived in England on a Kindertransport. Susi lived with guardians in Brackley, Northamptonshire, in central England.

Courtesy Susi Podgurski, Baltimore, Maryland, USA

LILLI VERA KRIEGER (NÉE JACOBSOHN)

Lilli left Berlin Bahnhof Zoo (the Berlin train station) in May 1939 on a Kindertransport to London, arriving at Liverpool Street Station.

Last picture, summer 1937, taken in Wengen, Switzerland, with Lilli's parents and sister (standing to the right). Lilli's mother is seated and Lilli is seated to her left.

Courtesy of Lilli Vera Krieger

Ernest was born in Eisenstadt, Austria, in May 1930. He and his family lived in the *Judengasse* (Jewish Lane), a self-imposed ghetto with a chain at each end to prevent vehicles from passing through during the period from the eve of the Sabbath (Friday evening) until the end of the Sabbath, (Saturday evening) after which the chain was removed. The Nazis created hundreds of ghettos in Eastern Europe, in Poland and Russia with the simple objective of gathering together the Jews of the town or neighborhood to enable them to put into effect the 'final solution' – the total extermination of Jews in Europe. In Eisenstadt, however, the Jewish ghetto was self-imposed. The Jewish population actually wanted to live in an area that would allow them to practice their religious observances without hindrance.

The history of the Jews in Eisenstadt goes back several hundred years. It is well known as a place of Jewish learning, where Jews were an integral part of the community. Ernest can trace his own family history back to 1805 on his father's side. His great-great-great-grandfather, Rabbi Yitzchak Tachauer, was born in Eisenstadt. His mother was born some sixty or seventy kilometers east of Eisenstadt in Hungary, in a small village near Sopron. She was the daughter of the village shoemaker, one of thirteen siblings. She went to work in Austria as a young woman and that is where she met Ernest's father. They married in 1928 and settled in Eisenstadt.

After the German *Anschluss* of March 1938, life changed. The Nazis' objective was to rid Austria of Jews. The entire Jewish community was forced to leave Eisenstadt in September 1938. Ernest and his family moved to Vienna, where they settled into a smallish flat in the Jewish quarter. During this time, his father was making desperate efforts to obtain an exit visa by applying to England, the United States and Palestine. Ernest's father was imprisoned, but fortunately released after two weeks.

Then there was Kristallnacht, when it became abundantly clear that all Jewish people were in immediate danger. Within three weeks after Kristallnacht, the Kindertransport movement was formed in the United Kingdom. Ernest, aged eight, said goodbye to his family, who didn't know if they would ever see him again, and left on a Kindertransport train from Vienna West Station at midnight on January 11, 1939. Ernest traveled through Germany and the Netherlands to the Hook of Holland, from where he and all the other youngsters on his transport were put on a ship for Harwich.

Ernest's younger brother stayed behind with his parents. Happily they were able to obtain a UK visa, which enabled them to come to England one month later, the condition being that they worked as domestic servants.

Ernest settled down with a very kind and welcoming Jewish family in Leeds in northern England and went to the local elementary school, not speaking a word of English. Fortunately, one of the teachers was Jewish and spoke a few words of Yiddish, which is similar to German. As a young child he picked up his 'new' language and within just a few weeks he was speaking English. His parents lived in Yeadon, in the city of Leeds, working as domestic servants for two doctors, and he was able to see them regularly. His younger brother lived with Jewish foster parents very nearby.

At the outbreak of World War II, Ernest was evacuated to Lincolnshire to live with a kind farming family in a relatively small village. Absolutely no German was spoken so his English improved and his German deteriorated. After Ernest had been there for some four months, his parents came to visit. Although his father's English had improved, his mother's had not, and this presented communication difficulties. She spoke in German, which Ernest understood, but he responded back in English, which she could not understand. This was very sad for his mother, who felt unable to communicate with her son and so she insisted he return to Leeds, which he did. After some six months in Lincolnshire he came back to Leeds and went to live in a hostel for refugee children together with his brother, who by then was aged seven and the youngest child in the hostel.

Around this time, his father was interned in the Isle of Man as an enemy alien along with many Jewish refugees from Germany and Austria. He spent about a year there. Since Austria had been annexed by Nazi Germany it was now considered to be the enemy, and since his father's nationality was Austrian, he too was the enemy. The fact that he was a Jewish refugee was totally immaterial. However, in 1941, Ernest's father was released and he came back to Leeds. He started to work in munitions production while his mother remained in domestic service. By 1941 they were all living together again as a family in a small house. Ernest spent his school years at Cockburn High School in south Leeds. Both Ernest and his brother had a very good school education. They both went to Leeds University. His brother studied medicine and became a doctor – a consultant anesthetist – and Ernest took a degree in economics and went into business.

Ernest's career spanned thirty-three years with ICI. He was the general manager of ICI's business in Hungary during the period 1987-1990, which was the last three years of the Soviet regime, just before the Wall came down.

Today Ernest is a hugely popular speaker in adult organizations, such as Rotary Clubs, and in schools under the auspices of the Holocaust Educational Trust (HET). He speaks annually at the Northwood United Synagogue and Northwood and Pinner Liberal Synagogue.

Text extracts courtesy of Ernest Simon, Pinner, UK

RUTH BARNETT

MARTIN MICHAELIS

Ruth Michaelis was born in Berlin in 1935. In 1939, when she was four years old, she came to England on a Kindertransport with her seven-year-old brother Martin. Over the next ten years, they lived with three foster families and in a hostel. Her father, who was Jewish, escaped to Shanghai. Her mother, who was not Jewish, remained in Germany in hiding until 1945. Ruth's mother had gone into hiding in 1943 because she had taken part in the Rosenstrasse protest in central Berlin. About 6,000 non-Jewish women who were married to Jewish men took part in this protest, which succeeded in obtaining the release of their Jewish husbands from prisons and concentration camps. Most of the men went on to survive the war.

In 1947 Ruth's father returned to Germany and wanted her to go and live with him. Ruth wanted to stay in England but was returned against her will by a subpoena served by her father. Ruth found this very traumatic, as she had once again lost the security of the home and country she had become used to. Her parents allowed her to return to England and visit them in Germany during the school holidays.

After leaving university, Ruth married her Jewish boyfriend and converted to Judaism. They celebrated their golden wedding anniversary in 2008 and have three children and two grandchildren. Ruth was a secondary school teacher for nineteen years and a psychotherapist for over thirty years. She regularly shares her testimony in schools and colleges and has written two books: *Person of No Nationality* and *Jews & Gypsies, Myths & Reality*.

Berlin, Germany

Text courtesy of the Holocaust Educational Trust, London, UK

SOFIE FRIEDMAN (NÉE SOMMER)

RUTH SOMMER

Sofie and Ruth came to England on a Kindertransport in 1939. Sofie received her nursing diploma in London in 1945, shortly before leaving for the United States.

Courtesy Sofie Friedman, Sherman Oaks, California, USA

KAETHE KLEIN

ROBERT 'BERTEL' KLEIN

LUDWIG KLEIN

HANNA KLEIN

WALTER KLEIN

All five Klein siblings left Bad Neustadt Saale, Germany, in August 1939, arriving in England a couple of days later. Kaethe was aged twelve, Bertel (Robert) aged fourteen, Ludwig aged thirteen, Hanna aged eleven and Walter aged three and a half. They were taken in by a sponsor. The four oldest went to a boarding school and Walter, the youngest, was sent away to a nursery. They were reunited one year later. Their parents did not survive the war.

Bad Neustadt Saale, Germany

Courtesy of Walter Klein, Liberty, New York and Delray Beach, Florida, USA

Train 57

RUTH HALOVA (NÉE ADLEROVA)

Ruth was born in 1926 in Český Krumlov, a small city in the South Bohemian region of Czechoslovakia. Ruth left on a Kindertransport organized by Nicholas Winton in July 1939.

CHILD A WINTON

Courtesy of Ruth Halova, Holubov, Czech Republic

Ruth was born on December 31, 1923, just moments before the clock struck midnight and the year turned 1924. Her father worked for the Nuremberg branch of the family wholesale/retail textile business. Her mother was a chemist. She had a very happy childhood until she was around ten years of age. Because of the growing anti-Semitism, she did not attend a German high school. She managed to get a place at a very good Jewish high school and graduated from there at the age of sixteen.

After Kristallnacht, her brother, who was three years her junior, managed to leave and went to Palestine, where many of her relatives lived. Ruth was given a place on a Kindertransport and left Berlin with a train full of youngsters. She remembers being harassed by a Nazi officer who came through to her cabin and took her watch. In Holland, she and the youngsters were treated with kindness and were given hot chocolate. When she finally arrived in England, she was taken in by a Jewish family. She lived with them for a year and a half until the outbreak of World War II, by which time she spoke very good English. She was interned on the Isle of Man because she was sixteen years old and considered an enemy alien.

After her internment, Ruth moved to London and worked for the defense industry. One day a member of the British royal family came to visit the factory. She was filled with great pride and, in her excitement, she for one moment lost her focus and cut her finger rather badly on the machinery.

Ruth heard from a cousin of her mother's who lived in Sweden that her parents had been deported to Sobibor and, within a few weeks of their deportation, had been gassed.

On January 1, 1947, Ruth arrived in the United States. Soon after, in March 1947, she married her second cousin (also a Heiman), who was ten years her senior and whose father was in the same textile business as her father. They had two children – a son and a daughter – and grandchildren.

Courtesy of Michael Heiman, Professor of Environmental Studies & Geography, Dickinson College, Carlisle, Pennsylvania, USA

CHARLOTTE COHEN (NÉE RINALHEIMER)

Charlotte with a group of young Jewish refugee girls on the way to a Kindertransport.

Courtesy of Charlotte Cohen, New York, New York, USA

BERTEL HERTZ (NÉE ROSENHEIN)

Bertel was born in Leipzig, Germany. She left Leipzig on the first Kindertransport out of Berlin, arriving in England on December 2, 1938.

Courtesy of Bertel Hertz, Valley Stream, New York, USA

LIESE B. FISCHER (NÉE EINSTEIN)

SIEGBERT EINSTEIN

Liese and her brother Siegbert were born in Augsburg, Germany. They were sent to England in July 1939. Their dear parents perished in Auschwitz circa 1943.

When the war broke out in September 1939, Liese was fourteen. She started working as a maid. Soon schools were closed. Siegbert started to feel very unwell with a fever and soon his condition worsened. On Liese's fifteenth birthday on February 26, 1940, he died. He was just sixteen years old.

Courtesy of Liese B. Fischer, Silver Spring, Maryland, USA

Train 58

SUSIE WEINBERG

CHARLOTTE WEINBERG

MARTIN WEINBERG

RUTH WEINBERG

Susie was twelve years old, Charlotte was nine and Ruth was four when they left Germany on a Kindertransport to England. Martin, aged six, did not leave with them; he left on the very last Kindertransport out of Germany.

Courtesy of Bayla Perrin (Charlotte's daughter) London, UK

Alfred (known as Freddy), an only child, was born in June 1925 in the town of Montabaur (near Koblenz), Germany. It was after Alfred's Bar Mitzvah, in the summer of 1938, that things became very difficult for him at school in Montabaur. He was one of a few Jewish children and was the subject of constant abuse and victimization – so much so, he was given a truncheon to take to school. He recalls a teacher strongly advising him and his family to leave Germany. He was taken out of school in Montabaur and sent to a Jewish boarding school in Bad Nauheim. He was actually at this school on Kristallnacht, and he escaped into an open doorway from a party of children who were rounded up at the school.

He was just thirteen years of age when he left on a Kindertransport, arriving in England on March 23, 1939. Alfred's parents, Willi and Betty Stern of Montabaur, and his grandparents, David and Rosa Loewenstein of Herborn, were all murdered. As many as 142 members of Alfred's family perished.

Courtesy of Gerald W. Stern, Newcastle upon Tyne, UK

Bertha was born in Munich, Germany, in January 1923. She was the eldest of three children. She came from a loving, Orthodox Jewish family and attended a Jewish school. Following Kristallnacht, her father Moishe Engelhard heard a rumor that there were transports to England for unaccompanied children. After pleading with the

Train Fifty-Eight

Jewish organizers who had their own lists of children, he managed to get Bertha and her brother Theo a place on a Kindertransport to England. There was a promise of her younger sister being able to be sent a few months later.

When they arrived in England in January 1939, Bertha was fifteen and Theo was twelve. They were sent to Dovercourt camp near Harwich and from there she was sent to be a maid to a childless non-Jewish couple in Coventry. Her sister Inge was sent later to the same cou-

ple, who earned payment for 'looking after' the children.

The children were not allowed to communicate with each other in their mother tongue and had minimal contact with other Jewish people or children who shared their plight. They bravely wrote to their parents, who had escaped to Yugoslavia and then Portugal, that they were fine and that their parents should not worry about them. An example of their ill treatment is when Theo broke his ankle, he was not believed by their carers until it was highly obvious that medical treatment was needed. Fortunately, their parents escaped the Nazis and they were all reunited in England in 1944. While this was also not without its hardships – Inge had forgotten her German and could not communicate with her parents who could not speak English – a new, happier era started.

Bertha married and raised a family. She has two daughters and ten grandchildren and great-grandchildren. Sadly, she lost a wonderful son at the age of twenty-one.

Bertha is the founder of the reunion of the Kindertransport and has dedicated a large part of her life to working tirelessly to keep the memories and stories alive. In 2005 she was awarded an MBE for her services and dedication to the Jewish people. The play *Kindertransport* is based on her family's story.

Courtesy of Bertha Leverton, Samaria, Israel

Inge was born on January 24, 1930, in Munich, Germany. She had two older siblings: a sister, Bertha, born in 1923, and a brother, Theo, born in 1927. She attended the Jewish school in Munich from September 1936 until it closed in November 1938.

After Kristallnacht, the children attended makeshift schools and many were registered for the Kindertransport to England. Bertha and Theo departed on January 4, 1939. Inge, who had only just turned nine, was put on a waiting list for a later transport. In June 1939, when the family was turned out of their apartment, Inge was placed with a mixed German-Jewish couple, while her parents were given shelter in the Jewish hospital. The following month, Inge was given a place on a Kindertransport that included children from Munich, Vienna, Frankfurt and Cologne.

Leaving on July 6, 1939, the children traveled by train to Holland and by boat to Harwich. When she arrived in England, Inge was taken to Coventry, where she was met by Bertha. Before giving consent to accepting Inge, Bertha's guardian had asked what color hair Inge had, as he had an immense hatred for ginger hair. Bertha realized that he would never have given permission to accept Inge had he known she was ginger and so she lied to him and said that Inge's hair was brown just like her own. When they arrived at the guardians' home, they were severely spanked for this lie but this was worth it for the fact that Inge had safely been brought to England. She stayed with Bertha's guardians for the next five years and Theo eventually moved in with them as well.

During the Blitz the children moved with their guardians to Delph in Yorkshire for part of the war, but mostly they were in Coventry, which was the most severely bombed city and they became used to dodging the bombs and taking gas masks everywhere. Though the children were grateful to be together, they were not treated warmly by their guardians.

Finally, in the early fall of 1940, they received a Red Cross communication informing them that their parents had succeeded in crossing over the Austrian mountains into Yugoslavia, where they remained until the German invasion in the spring of 1941. They then fled with the help of a Vatican priest who supplied them with the necessary documents. They escaped to Spain. Six months later they traveled illegally to Portugal, where they stayed until December 1943. On Christmas Day they got passage on the Yankee Clipper and flew to Britain, where they were reunited with their children. However the reunification was not ideal, as Inge was not able to communicate with her parents as she had forgotten how to speak German and her parents did not speak English. Furthermore, the family had to reunite on a different cultural path that had widened during the five years of the war and the different types of suffering that all members of the family had undergone.

United States Holocaust Memorial Museum,
photo courtesy of Inge Engelhard Sadan

RUTH ATLAS (NÉE EICHTERSHEIMER)

Ruth arrived on a Kindertransport from Germany to Coventry, England.

Newspaper photograph of Ruth's arrival in 1939 in Coventry. Ruth is on the far right.

Five Jewish refugees reached Coventry last night direct from Germany. Picture shows them on arrival at the station with Mr. Maurice Cohen, President of the Coventry Hebrew Congregation, who, with his daughter (extreme left), met the girls in London and traveled with them here.

Courtesy of Ruth Atlas, Granada Hills, California, USA

Ernest and other refugee children, taken as they arrived in Paris

Ernest Marx was the son of Siegmund and Bertha (née Steinberger) Marx. He was born in 1925 in Gelnhausen, Germany. In 1927 his family moved to Rothenberg and in 1933 moved again to Speyer, where his father worked as a religious teacher and cantor before receiving his rabbinical ordination in 1936. Ernest had one older brother, Julius, who was born in 1922. Ernest's father was arrested during Kristallnacht, November 9, 1938, and he was told to bring along one son. It was quickly decided that Ernest would go with him and his brother Julius would stay behind to look after his mother. Ernest and his father were sent to Dachau for six weeks, during which time Ernest celebrated his Bar Mitzvah. Shortly after their release, Julius was sent to Switzerland and Ernest was sent to France on a Kindertransport.

Sometime towards the end of 1939 the Marx family received American immigration visas, but they were never able to use them to leave Europe. Ernest's father was arrested in September 1939 as a German enemy alien and sent to Saint Germain, in France. The following summer after the fall of France, he was rearrested as a foreign-born Jew and imprisoned in the Les Milles internment camp. In 1942 he was transferred to Drancy and from there, he was deported to his death in Auschwitz.

Ernest's mother eluded arrest and in 1942 was living in hiding in Limoges, France. Ernest was able to join her there in 1942, but shortly after their reunion they were both arrested separately and sent to the Gurs internment camp, where they were unaware of each other's presence. Ernest managed to escape from the camp with four friends. Ernest joined up with the *Chasseur Alpin*, a unit of the French 'Maquis' resistance. Ernest's mother remained in Gurs and was slated for transfer to Drancy when she suffered a stroke and was left for dead. Miraculously, she recovered and survived the rest of the war. After the war Ernest and his mother were reunited with Julius, who had remained in Switzerland throughout the war. After Ernest completed his military service in the French army, the surviving members of the Marx family immigrated to the USA.

United States Holocaust Memorial Museum, courtesy of Ernest L. Marx

Train 59

WALTER WEG

Walter was born in Leipzig, Germany, in November 1928. His family had been German for several generations. His father, together with his two brothers, ran a book publishing business. Walter and his two younger sisters went to a Jewish kindergarten organized by a circle of Jewish friends.

After Hitler came to power in 1933, an increasing number of restrictions were placed on Jews. Walter remembers things getting worse still from 1936: rudeness and insults in the streets; many shops had 'Jews not welcome' notices; he was unable to go to the cinema, and the family found they could no longer go on holiday.

The Jewish school he attended was a two-tram ride away from home. Walter remembers the morning after Kristallnacht, when he found broken glass scattered over the pavements, and the road covered with half-burned school books. He returned to the tram stop a different way and saw damaged and looted Jewish shops. Three days later the SS came and took away his father. Fortunately Walter's mother managed to go to the Gestapo HQ in Leipzig and get her husband released from the Sachsenhausen concentration camp. They were all shocked by his broken appearance when he returned home. One of Walter's uncles died in the camp, but another uncle managed to have his own family join him in Holland.

At this stage Walter's mother decided to send the three children away and an English businessman agreed to take Walter with him when he returned to London. He was fortunate to be sent to a boarding school in Hastings. He was later evacuated to Devon.

Walter's two sisters came to the UK on the Kindertransport in February 1939 and his mother got out of Germany in July 1939. His father could not get the right papers until the end of August and he left at once to join Walter, who was with the uncle and family in Holland. With World War II imminent, Walter and his father left the next morning for England. The family planned to go on to America, but could not get on any ships, so they remained in England throughout the war and became British citizens in 1949.

Sadly, when the Nazis invaded Holland, the Dutch uncle and his family were put into a concentration camp, and then moved to Theresienstadt and finally Auschwitz, where Walter's uncle and aunt and their two sons perished.

Happily a girl cousin survived. She is now a great-grandmother and lives in Israel.

Text extracts courtesy of HMD (Northwood Holocaust Memorial Day Events)

GERDA SCHWARTZ

Gerda was a young Jewish refugee girl who arrived on a Kindertransport to England and spent time at the Whittingehame *Hachshara* training farm.

Courtesy of the United States Holocaust Memorial Museum

Ben was born in December 1925 in Kolomyja, Poland. At just five years of age, he left Poland to live with his uncle and aunt in Breslau, Germany. His sister was already there. His uncle and aunt were childless. He attended a Jewish school until Kristallnacht, November 9, 1938. All his school teachers were arrested and taken to concentration camps and his school virtually came to a standstill. In early December 1938 he heard that there was a committee with which one could register for emigration and he enrolled. Early in 1939 he heard that there might be a place for him to go to Sweden. This fell through. Then a few months later, in May 1939, he heard there might be a place for him in Holland, but this also fell through.

On August 27, 1939, he was told there was a place in England and he left Breslau on August 30 for Berlin, staying in a synagogue there overnight, and then, the following morning, he made his way to the station to take

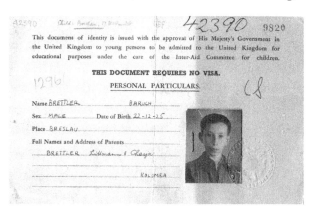

the train to Holland. This was the only border open. There was a deferment until midday, when the children were allowed to leave on the promise to the Dutch government that the transport would be permitted to enter England, should war break out in the interim. Ben arrived in England September 1, 1939. He stayed overnight in London and from there he went on *Hachshara* to Bydown in Swimbridge, Devon. He stayed there until November 1941, when he moved to London. In London he lived in a hostel and found various jobs to support himself until 1944, when he was called up to serve in the Polish Army.

Text courtesy of Ben and Judith Brettler, Wilmslow, Cheshire, UK

Rella was the daughter of Isaac and Klara Hudes. She was born in September 1931 in Vienna, where her father worked as a cabinetmaker. She had one brother, Siegmund, who was born in 1923. Rella's father went to Palestine, where he remained until his death from natural causes in 1942. The rest of the family stayed in Vienna. In 1939 arrangements were made to send Rella to Holland, where she was to stay with a family, but it was decided that she should go to England to live with a couple in Sheffield. She left on a Kindertransport from Vienna and arrived at the home of Lilian and Philip Adams on June 31, 1939, and remained with them until 1947. During this entire period Rella had no communication with her family in Vienna. In 1947 Lilian Adams contacted the Jewish Refugee Committee requesting information on the fate of Rella's relatives. The response confirmed that her mother and brother had been deported from Vienna in 1943 and had perished. Shortly after hearing this news, Rella was contacted by her aunt Ida who arranged for her to come to New York to live with her.

Vienna City Hall

Courtesy of the United States Holocaust Memorial Museum, Rella Hudes Adler

Train 60

HARRY HEBER (FORMERLY HEINZ)

RUTH JACOBS (NÉE HEBER)

Harry and his sister Ruth were born in Vienna. Harry was seven and Ruth was ten when they left Vienna in mid-December, 1938, on a Kindertransport to England.

Courtesy of Harry Heber, London, UK

Harry was born in June 1929 in Munich, Germany, and Sammy was born in August 1933 in Berlin. In June 1939 Harry and Sammy left Berlin on a Kindertransport, most likely via Hamburg, sailing on the *SS Bremen*. They arrived at Southampton on June 14, 1939, from where they traveled the final lap of their journey by train to London. They were met by the eldest son of the Jewish family in Nottingham with whom Harry was to live for the next six years. Sammy lived with friends of this family, also in Nottingham. They stayed with their respective families until 1945, when the two brothers moved to London and were reunited with their father, who managed to get to England in 1944.

Courtesy of Harry Kornhauser, London, UK

Train Sixty

VERA COPPARD-LEIBOVIC

(née Ilse Vera Rosendorff)

Vera was born in Berlin in 1926. On May 23, 1939, when she was twelve years old, she left on a Kindertransport arriving at the port of Dover, England, via the Hook of Holland.

Berlin bridge

Courtesy of Vera Coppard-Leibovic,
Buffalo, New York, USA

ALEXANDER KLEIN

Alexander was born in Vienna in October 1924. In May 1939 he left from Vienna on a Kindertransport via Brussels, and then he went from the French port of Calais to Dover, England, by ferry. He finally arrived in London by train. He was fifteen years old.

Courtesy of Diane Spender (daughter),
London, UK

HELGA SHEPARD (NÉE USZEROWICZ)

Helga was born in August 1932 in Berlin. She had an older brother, Martin, who was born in May 1923. In May 1939 Helga and Martin left Berlin on a Kindertransport to England. Helga first stayed with a family in Nottingham. She left them during the Blitz, when she was evacuated to Oxford. Helga returned to Nottingham in 1942, the same year that her brother Martin tragically drowned at the age of eighteen. Helga left for boarding school in 1945. In 1947 she was reunited with her parents in Paris. They had both survived: her father spent the war in Shanghai and her mother was liberated in Italy, following an incarceration in the Gurs internment camp in France.

United States Holocaust Memorial Museum,
courtesy of Helga Shepard

GERTI URMAN LAVI

Gerti was eleven years old when she left Vienna in April 1939 to go to England on a Kindertransport.

Natural History Museum, Vienna

Courtesy of Gerti Urman Lavi, Lower Galilee, Israel

Train 61

Jewish refugee girls arriving in England on a Kindertransport.

*Photo courtesy of The Wiener Library
for the Study of the Holocaust & Genocide, London, UK*

JOSEF BACZELES

BERTA BACZELES

WALTER SOBOLKA

Berta and her brother Josef left Vienna on December 10, 1938, on a Kindertransport to Hull, in Yorkshire, England, arriving on December 12, 1938. Berta was eight years old and her brother was thirteen. Pictured with them is Walter Sobolka, one of the other children who arrived on this transport.

Courtesy of Pearl and Graham Aaronson, London, UK

ALBERT STERNBERG

Albert was born in Prostějov, Czechoslovakia. At seventeen years of age, he just made the age allowance when he left on a Kindertransport in 1939. He married in the UK and has two sons and one daughter.

Courtesy of Dov Bronfman, Netanya, Israel

ROSELIND BAUM (NÉE ROSI BERLINGER)

Roselind was born in Schweinfurt, Germany, in 1928. She had one sister, Senta, who was seven years older. Their parents were Asher (Artur) and Berta Berlinger. The family lived in the two-story building of the Schweinfurt Jewish Community Council, occupying one half of the upper floor. The other half was occupied by the local rabbi and his family. Schweinfurt had a population of about 40,000 and approximately 350 Jewish people living there. Her father was the cantor at the synagogue as well as the teacher of the Jewish community. He taught a wide range of subjects: from Hebrew to music and art. He was also an accomplished artist in fine and graphic arts, and sculpturing. Roselind attended public school for a few grades, but was expelled because she was Jewish and subsequently she attended a one-room school operated by the Jewish community. Her father was the teacher. During Kristallnacht, the synagogue adjacent to their home was looted and set on fire. Their home was ransacked and severely damaged and a fire was started on the lower level of their building. Shortly after this, her father was arrested and sent to the Dachau concentration camp. He was released after more than one month, most likely because of his military service as a front line soldier during World War I.

In early 1939, when she was eleven years old, Roselind was sent on a Kindertransport to England. There were about 200 other children on the train. She was met at Liverpool Street Station by her foster parents, an Orthodox Jewish couple, who lived in the East End of London and had three children of their own. She was very well treated and accepted by all the family. Following several evacuations from London to small towns during air raids, and the destruction by bombs of her foster parents' home, Roselind's foster father died in a tragic accident. Feeling that she was too much of a burden, Roselind left her foster family voluntarily and went to live in a hostel. At a social function she met her husband-to-be, Henry (Heinz), who had also come to England on a Kindertransport. Roselind remained in close contact with her foster mother and still communicates with her children.

In 1948 Roselind came to the United States, thanks to the efforts of a cousin who already lived there. Henry had preceded her and they were married in 1949. Roselind moved from New York to Detroit, where he had settled. They have two sons and one daughter, as well as grandchildren and great-grandchildren. They both continue to practice their Orthodox Jewish faith, which was instilled in them by their parents during early childhood and has continued on in their children, grandchildren and great-grandchildren.

Courtesy of Roselind Baum (Rosie Berlinger Baum), Southfield, Michigan, USA

Kurt was born in Vienna in 1925. In 1939 he left Vienna on a Kindertransport to England. Kurt has always been a dedicated member of his community. He served as past President of the Kindertransport Association of North America from 1999-2012. Kurt is on the Governing Board of the World Federation and is the former Vice President of the World Federation of Jewish Child Survivors. Professionally, Kurt worked briefly for the Anti-Defamation League of B'nai B'rith and subsequently he spent twenty years as a regional director of District One B'nai B'rith. After his retirement he worked briefly as a fundraiser for UJA/Federation of Long Island. He has also served as chair of the Long Island B'nai B'rith Youth Organization and is a member of the board of the B'nai B'rith House (for senior citizens) in Queens, New York.

Vienna

Courtesy of Kurt Goldberger, Hicksville, New York, USA

Train 62

HILDE STEINHART (NÉE AUERHAHN)

Hilde was born in Leipzig, Germany, in March 1921. Her mother Rosa died in 1931. Her elder brother Yosef left for Palestine with Youth Aliyah in 1936. Her father Yisrael remarried and in December 1938 he and his second wife Adele had a son, Jacob. In February 1939 Hilde left Germany for London on a Kindertransport.

Her father, step-mother and young brother were in internment camps in Tuscany in Italy and were arrested in Lucca in November 1943. In January 1944 they were transported to Auschwitz, where they were murdered.

Hilde's aunt and uncle, Ella and Rudi Danzig, came to London from Leipzig shortly before the war and she lived with them in northwest London. She married Alf Steinhart in 1948 and they had two daughters and five grandchildren. After the terrible losses she suffered when she was young, Hilde treasured her own very happy marriage and family life. Hilde died in 1996.

My Mother's Photo Album
By Marian Lebor, May 2014

At the bottom of a drawer in my mother's bedroom there was an album full of sepia photographs. As a young girl I sometimes took it out and looked at it and wondered who all the people were. But I had learnt over time not to show it to my mother and ask her about it, because her eyes would immediately fill with tears.

Hilde with her mother
Rosa Auerhahn

My mother left Germany in February 1939, one month before her eighteenth birthday, so she just made it on to the Kindertransport. Like all the other young refugees, she was allowed only one small suitcase in which she could put some clothes and special belongings – like her photo album.

She rarely spoke about her childhood in Leipzig, her experience on the Kindertransport, or what it was like living as a refugee in wartime London. I always thought that one day she would tell me more about her life, or perhaps tell my own children as they grew up. It's quite common that people talk more readily to their grandchildren rather than their children about their wartime experiences. But my mother died suddenly in 1996 while they were still young.

So my sister and I have tried to piece together her family story by speaking to surviving relatives, and by tracking down books that document the lives of the Jews who perished. A few years ago, we discovered in a book of memory published in Italy that my grandparents and Jacob were in internment camps in Tuscany and that they were arrested in Lucca on November 30, 1943. They were transported to

Auschwitz on train number six on January 30, 1944, and were 'alive for the last time on February 6, 1944', when Jacob was five years old.

Now we knew that Jacob was born barely one month after Kristallnacht, which was one of the very few things about her life in pre-war Germany that my mother ever spoke about. She described the horror of the night the Gestapo pounded on the door of her family's apartment, searching for her father. But we never realized that her young brother was barely two months old when she left.

We recently discovered that one of the photographs in our mother's album that had remained unidentified is in fact of our grandparents and Jacob taken in 1940, when they were being held in an internment camp in Milan. It is the only photo we have of Jacob Auerhahn, our uncle, who would have been seventy-five had he lived - just sixteen years older than me.

I often think of the utter despair my grandfather must have felt as he and his wife and their young son were herded onto train number six. He probably understood the fate that awaited them and could only hope that by allowing his teenage son to leave for an uncertain future in Palestine in 1936, and by putting his young daughter on a Kindertransport train in 1939, he had at least ensured their safety.

Adele and Yisrael Auerhahn
with their young son Jacob, March 1940.

Indeed he did, and between them they gave my grandfather seven grandchildren and many great-grandchildren and great-great-grandchildren. Almost all of them are today living in Israel.

Courtesy of Marian Lebor, Ra'anana, Israel, and Ros Sloboda, London, UK

RUTH ROSEN (NÉE KANNER)

EVE ROSENZWEIG KUGLER (NÉE KANNER)

Ruth was born in Germany in October 1929. Eve was born in Germany in 1931. In September 1939 Ruth and Eve entered the OSE Home on the outskirts of Paris. They were amongst a few hundred Kindertransport children who were residents of OSE homes in France who traveled to the United States on a special State Department Visa in 1941. OSE is a long established Jewish welfare organization that ran a number of homes in France for Jewish children who were displaced by the war. Many of the children who were saved on this Kindertransport, and by OSE working with the French Resistance, are members of the 'Friends and Alumni of OSE-USA'.

On the day of their departure for America in June 1941, the children were gathered on the steps of their OSE home in Haute in Vienne, France. Ruth is on the front step (wearing glasses) with her dear friend Frieda Rosenblum Grab (left), and her youngest sister Lea, aged just four and a half. Lea dashed to the front before the photo was snapped although she did not come with the group. Eve is behind Lea and her mother Mia is behind her. Their father Sal, wearing a French beret, is in the second row, far left.

Photo and text extracts courtesy of Eve R. Kugler and Mia Amalia Kanner, London, UK, authors of Shattered Crystals *http://www.shatteredcrystals.net*

Elisabeth was born in December 1925 in Eschersheim, near Frankfurt. She had two younger siblings: Lux, who was born in June 1927 and Agathe, who was born in July 1930. In June 1939 Elisabeth and Lux were sent to England on a Kindertransport. After their arrival both youngsters stayed with a family who were related to their dentist in Frankfurt.

After the war began this family could no longer care for Elisabeth and Lux, so they were separated. Lux went to Barham House in Claydon, a hostel for boys, and Elisabeth went to the Beacon in Rusthall. After three months she left to stay with the Goldstein family. Mrs. Goldstein had been a piano student of her father's in Germany. In May 1940 the Goldsteins had to evacuate their town, and the Woman's Voluntary Service needed to find a new home for Elisabeth. They referred her to Mrs. Hayes, and Elisabeth lived with her for the next few years.

Elisabeth earned her school certificate in 1941 and then went to a business school to study languages, bookkeeping and typing. In 1942 Lux also came to live with them after receiving his school certificate. Elisabeth and Lux's parents remained in Frankfurt until it was bombed and then moved to Zwingenberg.

In September 1945 Elisabeth received the first post-war letter from her family. She and Lux saw their parents and younger sister Agathe again for the first time in November 1947. In 1948 Lux and Elisabeth visited their family in Germany. Elisabeth became a British citizen. In 1949 their father became a judge in a Frankfurt court and later became president of the Senate. Elisabeth met her husband Kurt Reinhuber at the British Consulate in Frankfurt in 1950.

United States Holocaust Memorial Museum,
courtesy of Elisabeth Reinhuber-Adorno

R uth was born in Munich, Germany. She escaped with her cousin Bianca Bravmann on a Kindertransport in 1939. Ruth was the daughter of Gerda Danzig who perished at a very young age. Her aunt Flora brought Ruth over to the United States and adopted her.

The Great Synagogue of Munich, which Hitler ordered to be destroyed, June 1938.

United States Holocaust Memorial Museum, courtesy of Steven Frank

KURT FROST (LATER MORDECHAY)

K urt was the son of Alfred Frost and Regina Adler Frost. Kurt was born in 1927 in Vienna, where his father's family had lived since the 18th century. His mother's family came from Wadowice, Poland, and had settled in Vienna. Kurt's younger sister Gertrude was born in 1937. Life changed dramatically for them after the *Anschluss*, when his father's business was confiscated. His parents were anxious for them to all leave Austria. In January 1939 Kurt's parents sent him on a Kindertransport to Belgium. After a short stay in a children's home, a Belgian Jewish family took Kurt in as a foster child. He became the companion of this family's only child, a son Henri who was approximately the same age.

In September 1939 Kurt's parents and sister Gertrude fled to Belgium and settled in Antwerp. Kurt remained with the same family a while longer until his parents found housing and a job. Germany invaded Belgium on May 10, 1940, and the next day the Belgian authorities arrested his father as an enemy alien and deported him to Le Vernet internment camp in France. His mother decided to flee to France with both Kurt and Gertrude, but when they discovered German tanks at the border, they had no choice but to return to Antwerp. The following year the family received a deportation order. Rather than comply, Kurt's mother went to the German headquarters. Carrying her husband's World War I medals, she explained to the German commandant that her husband had served as an officer in the war and that she wanted to be allowed to reunite with him in France. The commandant granted permission for the family to travel.

Alfred, who was constructing roads on a nearby forced labor brigade, was allowed to rejoin them. In 1942, as the situation for Jews became more urgent, a woman visited them on behalf of Rabbi Fuchs. He was organizing transports for children to smuggle over the border to Switzerland in September 1942. The children were first sent to a refugee camp in Geneva. Gertrude was then placed in a convent while Kurt moved to Appenzell in Switzerland. From there, he moved to Les Murailles, a children's home in Geneva run by a Jewish woman, and he remained there for a couple of years.

In early 1943 Kurt's parents received a warning that they were about to be arrested and should flee immediately. They made their way to Nimes in southern France where they hired a *passeur* (ferryman) to take them to Switzerland. He brought them as far as he could. They managed to cross the border. The Swiss interned them in separate work camps, segregated by gender. After Kurt heard that his parents had arrived in Switzerland, he borrowed a bike and cycled over 100 kilometers to visit.

After the war Kurt's parents received permission to remain in Switzerland, owing to prewar business connections. They remained there for the rest of their lives. In July 1945 Kurt immigrated to Palestine. He joined the Palmach and fought in Israel's War of Independence and was wounded in the leg. After the war he helped found Kibbutz Yiftach in the Galil, in northern Israel. Kurt worked for the Jewish Agency, Hebrew University and Jewish National Fund.

United States Holocaust Memorial Museum, courtesy of Mordechay Frost

GIRLS IN THE DORMITORY

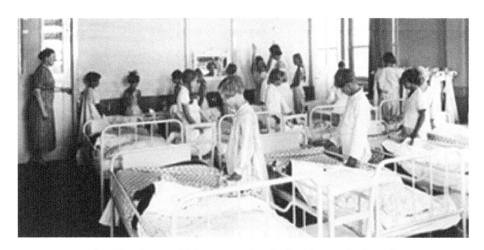

Jewish refugee children preparing for bedtime at the hostel.

United States Holocaust Memorial Museum,
courtesy of Ilse (Lichtenstein) Meyer

Pictured are four boys, Henri, Max, Egon and Kurt, in the Priory,
a children's home in Selkirk, Scotland.

United States Holocaust Memorial Museum, courtesy of Gunther Abrahamson

DAGMAR SIMOVA (NÉE DEIMLOVA)

Dagmar was born in Czechoslovakia in March 1928. Her sister Milena was born in December 1932.

In July 1939 Dagmar was supposed to be leaving on a Kindertransport. Her sister was also supposed to go, as they had both been 'selected' by a family with whom they would be staying. But her sister broke her leg, and so her parents made the decision not to send her anywhere until September, when it was thought she would have fully recovered. The September transport never left. The family that Dagmar and her sister were supposed to go to did not want to take Dagmar alone, they wanted siblings. It was then arranged with her uncles, who had already settled in England, that Dagmar would go to them.

Dagmar later left for England on one of the Winton trains. She traveled with her dearest lifelong friend Alice Klimova, who died in May 2009. Her transport label number was 298.

Courtesy of Dagmar Simova, Prague, Czech Republic

ALICE KLIMOVA (NÉE JUSTITZOVA)

Alice was born in 1928 in Prague. She was eleven years old when she arrived in England on one of Nicholas Winton's transports, traveling with her lifelong friend, Dagmar Simova.

Courtesy of Dagmar Simova, Prague, Czech Republic

Train 64

HERBERT LEVY

Herbert was born on July 28, 1929, in Berlin. In June 1939 Herbert was the youngest boy in the carriage when he left Berlin on a Kindertransport, traveling through the night via the Hook of Holland to Harwich, and then to Liverpool Street Station in London, where an uncle collected him.

He was in transit for America but after the war started all commercial shipping ceased, so he stayed in England and made it his home.

During the war he was interned as an enemy alien on the Isle of Man. He returned to the mainland but was still imprisoned in south London – just in time for the Blitz (the air attacks of the German Luftwaffe). Herbert survived them all and eventually did National Service in 1950 in the British Army Education Corps.

Herbert went on to become an actor and writer. His wife Lilian survived the Bergen-Belsen concentration camp.

Photo courtesy of Herbert Levy, London, UK, from his book Voices from the Past

Helga was born in 1927 in Stettin (now Szczecin), Poland. She and her family lived in an apartment in the town and also owned a small weekend bungalow just outside. Her father was the chief accountant of a large store where he had worked for many years. Trouble began in 1937, when the store's directors were accused of false accounting. The owner fled to Switzerland and her father, because he was Jewish, was sent to prison for a month. Even before this event, Helga remembered seeing notices outside hotels, restaurants and shops with wording such as 'Jews not allowed here' or 'Entry forbidden for Jews'. On one vacation to the Black Forest the family was turned away when they arrived just because they were Jewish. Frightened by such events, Helga's father found a job in Leipzig, Germany.

Helga remembers hearing Nazi boots tramping along the street. They stopped at the main door of their apartment block and then there was banging on the door. Helga's mother quickly turned all the lights off and Helga and her parents remained perfectly still. They heard them stop outside their door and then continue tramping upstairs to the flat above. The next morning, they heard that the Jewish gentleman who lived in the flat above them had been arrested.

Shortly after this Helga's father was arrested on his way to the barbershop, taken to the local police station and then transported to the Buchenwald concentration camp. Helga vividly remembers Kristallnacht, when synagogues and Jewish schools were burned to the ground. Everyone was laughing and joking about this shocking crime the Nazis had committed. Helga remembers her teacher telling her to go home quickly. All the books had been burned, windows broken and the headmaster arrested.

During the time Helga's father was held in Buchenwald for six long weeks, it was suggested that her mother should put her and her sister's names on the list of children able to leave the country. They left on the first Kindertransport to England in December 1938. On Monday, December 19, 1938, the Kindertransport full of Jewish refugee children arrived at Liverpool Street Station. Helga was met by her foster parents. She said a tearful goodbye to her sister and then she was driven away to her new home. Her foster parents treated her with great kindness.

Her father was released from the concentration camp – partly because he had served in the army during World War I and won several medals for bravery. Against all odds, Helga's foster parents managed to bring her parents out of Germany in May 1939 and they looked after Helga and her family until her mother was able to find work.

Stetton, Germany

Text extracts courtesy of Northwood Holocaust Memorial Day Event (NHMDE), Northwood, UK

HANS LOPATER

Hans was born in Vienna. In 1939 he left for England on a Kindertransport.

Photo courtesy of the Imperial War Museum, London, UK

REGINA ROSENBLATT

Regina found refuge in the children's home in Zuen, Brussels.

United States Holocaust Memorial Museum, courtesy of Walter Reed

KLARA NEMETH

Klara attended a school on the outskirts of Edinburgh that provided shelter for German and Austrian Jewish youth who came on the Kindertransport.

Courtesy of the United States Holocaust Memorial Museum.

ERIC KAY

(formerly Erich Sigmund Kahn)

Eric was born in November 1926 in Heidelberg, Germany. He left for England in the middle of 1939 on a Kindertransport via the Hook of Holland to Harwich, and finally he arrived in London. Once there, he was met by a member of his host family and taken to their home in Barrow-in-Furness in northern England. He was twelve and a half years old. After the war, in 1948, Eric left England for the United States. Nineteen members of Eric's extended family perished.

Courtesy of Eric Kay, Saratoga, California, USA

RONALD H. KAY

(formerly Heinz Julius Kahn)

Ronald was born in March 1923 in Heidelberg, Germany. He was three years older than his brother Eric. During the first half of 1939 Ronald left for England on a Kindertransport. He was sixteen years old. A year or so later he left England for the United States, where he joined the US Armed Forces and returned to Germany as a GI.

Courtesy of Eric Kay, Saratoga, California, USA

On September 1, 1939, some 250 children sat on a train in Prague Wilson Station awaiting their journey to Britain. But on this day, World War II began. The train departed, but not to its intended destination.

The fate of those children is unknown.

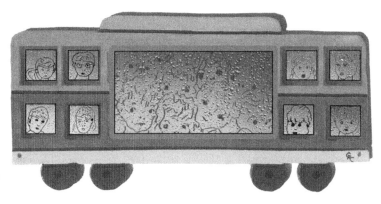

'The Train that Didn't Leave'

Ten thousand children were taken to safety
on the Kindertransport trains.

More than one million children
perished in the Holocaust.

ACKNOWLEDGEMENTS

I would like to reiterate my thanks to each and every one of the *kinder* and their families who sent me stories and photographs. My special thanks go to Gabriella Karin for her unique ceramic trains and for all her sketches that add detail and depth to the stories.

My sincere gratitude goes to the Los Angeles Museum of the Holocaust, United States Holocaust Memorial Museum, Yad Vashem Museum, Beth Emeth Bais Yeduda Synagogue in Toronto, the Leo Baeck Institute, Bundesarchiv – Federal Archives, Manchester Jewish Museum, Imperial War Museum, Museum of London, Jewish Museum London, the Wiener Library for the Study of the Holocaust and Genocide, Beth Shalom Holocaust Centre, London Jewish Cultural Centre, Holocaust Educational Trust, Northwood Holocaust Memorial Day Events and many more for all the photos and historical information they provided.

Every effort has been made to contact all copyright holders. I apologize for any inadvertent omissions that may have been made in this regard. If any copyright holder has been overlooked and/ or incorrectly identified we would be grateful to be notified of any correction that should be incorporated in future reprints or editions of this book.

I thank Judith Cohen at the United States Holocaust Memorial Museum for all her help, support and kindness. Thanks also to Caroline Waddell at the museum. I thank Dr. Vladamir Melamed at the Los Angeles Museum of the Holocaust for the advice he offered whenever needed, and to Samara Hutman for her constant support.

I am grateful to the Kindertransport Association, Melissa Hacker, Kurt and Margarete Goldberger, the Association of Jewish Refugees and Michael Newman for their assistance and support. Special thanks to the remarkable Alisa Tennenbaum, who heads the Kindertransport Association in Israel, for her help and dedication.

I thank Michael Berenbaum and Matej Mináč for their insightful contributions to the book.

Thank you to Stephen D. Smith, Mare and Charles Chadwick, Sonia Levitin, Philippa Ford, Marcia Perkin and the many individuals, too numerous to mention, for all their support and interest.

I am indebted to my editor, Marian Lebor, who spent untold hours working with me. I cannot thank her enough for her dedication, passion and invaluable contributions during every stage of this book. Thank you to Judi for making this introduction. I am grateful to S. Kim Glassman for designing the book with great sensitivity and flair and I thank Moshe Alon and all the team at Kotarim International.

Special thanks to my brother Melvin and sister-in-law Sharman and my family for the love, support and advice they always give me.

To my husband Larry – my best friend – thank you for your patience and constant reassurance.

And finally, to my mother who I loved dearly. I thank her for teaching me the true values of life that I try each day to live up to. I am saddened that I was unable to piece together some of the earlier part of her life with her, but I think she would have been proud that this book is dedicated to her and hundreds of other *Kinder*.

Michele M. Gold

Kinder Listed Alphabetically

H

J

K

S

Group Photos

About the Author

Michele M. Gold grew up in London and moved to Los Angeles in October 1991. Her mother was a Kindertransport survivor. Michele's passion is educating about the Holocaust, in particular the experiences of Jewish children who escaped Nazi persecution by means of the Kindertransport program. Michele is actively involved in numerous charitable organizations and is a volunteer educator at the Los Angeles Museum of the Holocaust. She speaks to audiences throughout the United States and worldwide.

About the Artist

Gabriella Y. Karin was born in Bratislava, Slovak Republic, and now lives in Los Angeles. By the age of fourteen, she had experienced the horrors of World War II and the Holocaust. For three years, she was hidden in a convent and then for nine months, Karol Blanar risked his life to provide her with a safe haven. After a career in the fashion industry, she began sculpting in clay and became an accomplished artist. Gabriella has turned her personal pain and suffering into works of art.

'Memories that Won't Go Away'

Lightning Source UK Ltd.
Milton Keynes UK
UKOW07f1251280116

267314UK00002B/5/P